A Stitch *in* Time

THE CLEVELAND GARMENT INDUSTRY

SEAN MARTIN

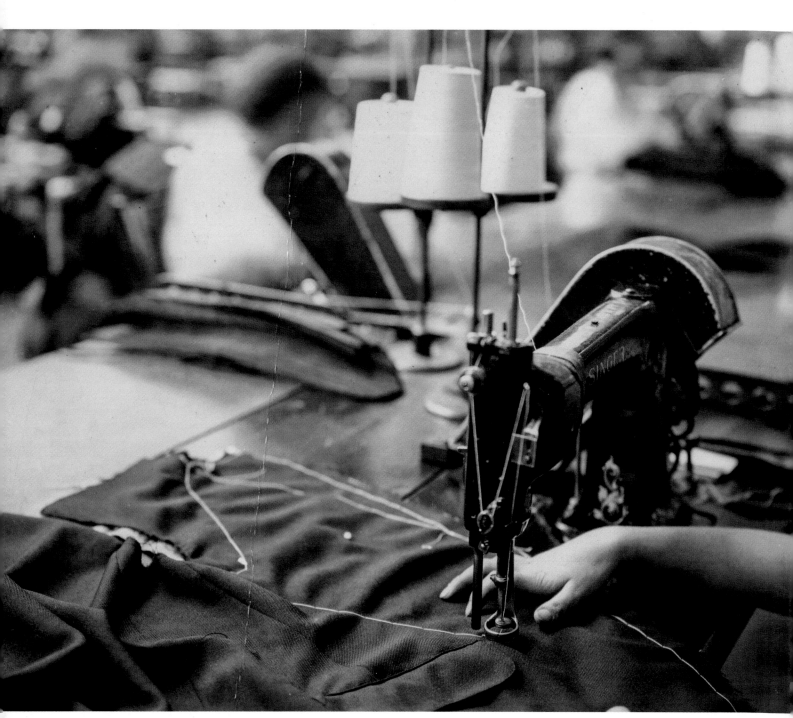

At Joseph & Feiss Company, undated. (Joseph & Feiss Company, WRHS)

A Stitch *in* Time

THE CLEVELAND GARMENT INDUSTRY

SEAN MARTIN

Published in the United States of America
The Western Reserve Historical Society

Design by Timothy Lachina
Walter Greene+Co.

Printed by Master Printing

The Western Reserve Historical Society Publication Number 198

ISBN 978-0-9967844-0-5

Captions, page 104-105, Left to right:

Office, Lattin-Bloomfield, ca. 1910. (WRHS)

Examining Department of Stone Knitting Mills, Christmas party, December 21, 1933. Photograph is mislabeled as Ohio Knitting Mills, not in existence until 1947. From bottom left, Benny Greenberg, shipping; unidentified woman; Harold Schwarz; Harry Stone; unidentified woman; Sophie Ziskin, head designer; Walker Woodworth. (Marc Frisch, WRHS)

Sidney Walzer is pictured in this photograph of the Executive Board of Cutters' Local 42, ILGWU, in 1941, on the occasion of the thirtieth anniversary of the existence of the local. Seated, left to right, S. Gordin, L. Zeman, Chairman, Joint Board, M. Berkman, President, Local 42, A. W. Katovsky, manager, Joint Board, L. Frieden, Business Agent, A. Wacher, Vice President, Local 42, Frank Rupp, Recording Sec., Local 42; standing, left to right, A. Goldbert, Y. Levine, A. Schlessinger, R. Smith, J. Wolstein, E. Freed, H. Keller, H. Haas, S. Walzer, I. Salzano.

Richard Adler at the opening of the new distribution center of Joseph & Feiss on Tiedeman Road, 1968. (Tom Adler, WRHS)

Herman Hager, Frisch Knitting Mills employee, presents Harry E. Frisch with a plaque recognizing 25 years in business, 1954. (Marc Frisch, WRHS)

Joseph Ehrlich, head buyer at Richman Brothers, 1950s-1960s. (Richard Reinberg)

Contents

FOREWORD

Some years ago, Nancy Schwartz, curator of the Cleveland Jewish Archives at Western Reserve Historical Society, asked my assistance to obtain information about the Cleveland knitwear industry and its members.

Several years after Nancy left the society, her place was taken by Sean Martin. He picked up the project, and we continued our mutual efforts. I had shared the idea with Gary Rand, who was enthusiastic, and our thoughts were to write and publish a book to include not only members of the knitwear group but the entire apparel industry, including suppliers.

It finally came to pass, whereby the Western Reserve Historical Society undertook the project, with John Grabowski leading and Sean Martin writing the manuscript.

Looking back, my time searching through the microfilm, finding new facts, participating in interviews, and meeting people within the industry has been an exciting and worthwhile venture. To know my efforts and contribution will end up in this history is of utmost satisfaction.

I am pleased to honor the memory of my father Harry E. Frisch of Frisch Knitting Mills, my brother Jerry Frisch, and my uncle Harry J. Stone of Stone Knitting Mills, who was Gary Rand's grandfather. We also remember Leonard Rand, Gary Rand's father, of Ohio Knitting Mills.

Gary has been instrumental in helping to coordinate the financial support for the project.

It is a wonderful history of the entrepreneurs, their employees and families, and their contribution to the growth and development of Cleveland.

Marc R. Frisch

From our factories to you, Richman Brothers, Louisville, Kentucky, 1930s. (Robert Harger, WRHS)

PREFACE

We at the Western Reserve Historical Society take great pride in the publication of *A Stitch in Time: The Cleveland Garment Industry.* It represents a major contribution to the history of Cleveland and Northeastern Ohio. Importantly, it brings to the forefront the story of the region's garment industry, a seminal player in its economic growth in the nineteenth and twentieth centuries, albeit one that often is overshadowed by a popular fascination with heavy industries such as iron, steel, and the manufacturing of automobiles. Yet, as Dr. Sean Martin's history amply illustrates, the business of making clothes was as central to Cleveland's national stature as were those other enterprises. Indeed, one could argue that it was a more personal enterprise, in that the skirts, jackets, trousers, and dresses produced in Cleveland found their way to the general population in a manner not really equaled by other local manufactured goods.

Yet, what makes this book particularly important for the Historical Society is the manner in which it weaves together multiple stories. Sean's text presents a story of individual vision, of the willingness to take risks, and of the vicissitudes that everyone who starts a business enterprise, large or small, must confront. But more so, it also contains the stories of workers, the neighborhoods in which they lived, and of a city that bustled with diversity and the interplay of people who had come to it looking for tolerance and opportunity. These stories are ones that the Historical Society has sought to preserve in its archival and museum collections. In bringing them to life, *A Stitch in Time* helps fulfill our mission not only to preserve the pieces and parts of the past, but to bring them back to life in images and text. For our staff, a book such as this, or an exhibit, or a lecture that derives from our holdings brings a satisfaction beyond measure.

Ultimately, what has made this book possible, and, of course, everything that the Western Reserve Historical Society does, is the trust of the community — a trust that places family heirlooms and business records with us, and a trust that provides both the enthusiasm and funding that allows us to support our staff and the projects that they undertake. The acknowledgments for this volume give a measure of the breadth of support, research assistance, and enthusiasm that made it possible. And while all are critical to what we do, perhaps it is enthusiasm that really makes a book like this possible. In this instance, Marc Frisch and Gary Rand stand at the core of this enterprise. Their commitment to telling the story of an industry that was part of their lives, as well as the lives of many of their friends and acquaintances, is what helped us knit together the history of Greater Cleveland's garment industry.

Kelly Falcone-Hall

President and CEO

The Western Reserve Historical Society

ACKNOWLEDGMENTS

This book would not be possible without the inspiration and support of Marc Frisch and Gary Rand. Special thanks are due to Cindy Bruml, a member of the Cleveland Jewish Archives Advisory Committee and the Western Reserve Historical Society Board of Directors. Her assistance in the research and preparation of the text, generous comments and continual encouragement throughout the process of writing and production were a tremendous help. WRHS interns Ruby Katz, Jessica Marra, Samuel Milner and Sebastian Wuepper helped to process collections related to the garment industry and also aided significantly in the research. John Grabowski, WRHS Historian, supervised this project from its initial stages and provided invaluable assistance throughout the research, writing, and production of the text.

The recent Chairs of the WRHS Cleveland Jewish Archives Advisory Committee, Sylvia Abrams, Ann Warren, and Sally Wertheim, graciously supported the project as part of the Committee's work to preserve and promote local Jewish history. Alan Gross of the Jewish Federation of Cleveland encouraged the project and offered guidance throughout the writing and production of the text.

Tom Adler, Marc Frisch, and Gary Rand were instrumental in helping to raise funds to support the writing and production of this book. Many others also helped with research questions and contributed comments and insights, including Harriett Applegate, Bob Bruml, Marianna R. Dostal, Jean Druesedow, David J. Goldberg, Gabriel Goldstein, Denise Grollmuss, Edie Hirsch, Steve Hoffman, Robert H. Jackson, Tim Lachina, Megan Spagnolo Lai, Stanley Lasky, Karen Long, Hanna Romaniuk, Richard Romaniuk, Clayton Ruminski, Edith Serkownek, Mark Souther, Roslyn Sugarman, Anne Trubek, Patricia Wren, and an anonymous reader. WRHS staff members Tim Beatty, Margaret Burzynski-Bays, Vicki Catozza, George Cooper, Pamela Dorazio Dean, Kelly Falcone-Hall, Hanna Kemp-Severence, Timothy Mann, Danielle Peck, Ed Pershey, Ann Sindelar, Mary Thoburn, and Dean Zimmerman also supported the research and writing in numerous ways.

Sean Martin

The following foundations and individuals contributed financially to make this history of the Cleveland garment industry a reality.

Stone Rand Philanthropic Fund	Mr. and Mrs. Kenneth Dery	Ms. Phyllis Melnick
Ruth G. and	Mrs. Patricia W. Dery	Ms. Donna Moss
Sam H. Sampliner Fund	Sheldon Fromson	Mrs. Richard Reinberg
Adler Family Foundation	Mr. and	Ms. Betty Rosskamm
William & Barbara Klineman	Mrs. Howard Garfinkel	
Philanthropic Fund	Armin Guggenheim	
Mr. and Mrs. Louis J. Bloomfield	Ms. Lenore Kessler	
Dave and Louise Butz	Mr. Stephen C. Lampl	

Those who worked for garment manufacturers, or whose families were involved in the industry, contributed significantly to this project by sharing their knowledge and experiences.

Tom Adler	Mary Hobbs	Ray Novak
James Anderson	Jane Horvitz	Gary Rand
John Bailey	Donald Jacobson	Charles Rosenblatt
Louise Lampl Butz	Fred Jones	Robert T. Rosenfeld
Ed Davis	Steve Kalette	Ileen Rosner
Ken Dery	Robert Kanner	Shirley Saltzman*
Robert Ebert	Jane Kaufman	Rita Saslaw
Marvin M. Epstein	Joan Kaufman	Alan Schoenberg*
Robert Flacks	Charlotte R. Kramer	Donald Shingler
Marc Frisch	Mike Klein	Bart Simon
Susan Gerdy	Bill Klineman	Ed Singer
Laura Goldstein-Wallenstein	Jeffrey Korach	Allison Stabile
Janet Reiter Greenberg	Carolyn Lampl	Mike Stern
Alan Gross	Stephen C. Lampl	Steve Tatar
Elaine Gross	Gregg Lurie	Ellen Vendeland
Louis N. Gross II*	Keith Lurie	Tony Zucker
Armin Guggenheim	Marge Mehes	Dan Zuckerman
Harry Guinther	Marjorie K. Miner	Kay Zuckerman
Bill Heller	Jeff Morris	*deceased

I

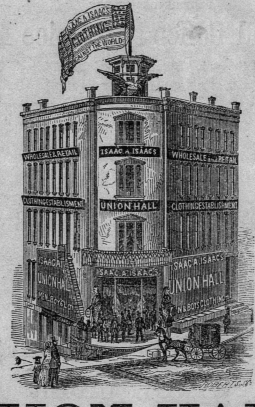

Advertisement for Isaac A. Isaac's Union Hall, 1863. (WRHS)

Advertisement for Joseph and Feiss. (Joseph & Feiss Company, WRHS)

Favorite Knitting Mills, 1388 West 6ᵗʰ Street.
(Howard Israel, Zweig Brothers Realty, WRHS)

Symbol of the Garment Industry. Simon Levy, Tailor, was born in Lithuania, emigrated to England and then to the United States in 1900. He continued as a tailor in Cleveland's garment industry for more than two decades. C. 1930. Photograph and caption from WRHS Jewish Heritage Exhibit (Benjamin B. Levy, Jewish Federation of Cleveland, WRHS)

Retail store selling men's clothing, from papers of former Richman Brothers executive. (Penny Wightman Dalzell, WRHS)

Rose, employee of Federal Knitting Mills on strike, 1937. (Richard S. Campen, WRHS)

Sponging machine, Joseph & Feiss, 1920. (Joseph & Feiss Company, WRHS)

Richman Brothers retail store. (Robert Harger, WRHS)

Bowling team of Richman Brothers, ca. 1920s. (Robert Harger, WRHS)

Overcoats produced for the military by Joseph and Feiss during World War II. (Joseph & Feiss Company, WRHS)

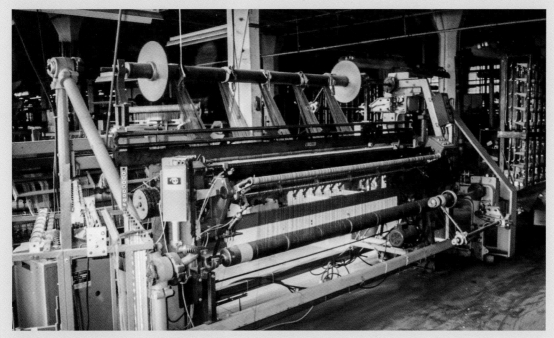

This machine, made by Caperdoni in Italy, made possible weaving and knitting at the same time. The only Caperdoni machines in the United States were at Ohio Knitting Mills. **2000s.** (Gary Rand, WRHS)

Richman Brothers beauty pageant winners Connie Barcinkowski and Evelyn Krejci with Frank C. Lewman, President of Richman Brothers in the 1940s. (Robert Harger, WRHS).

Harry Stone, of Stone Knitting Mills. (Gary Rand, WRHS)

INTRODUCTION

What can you spare that they can wear?

THAT WAS THE QUESTION ASKED OF CLEVELANDERS AT THE END OF WORLD WAR II. Europe's refugees were in desperate need, and community organizations came together to provide aid to refugees in Central and Eastern Europe. Local leaders organized a clothing drive in cooperation with national groups and representatives of the area's immigrant populations. The United National Clothing Collection sponsored what became an interethnic effort, involving many different kinds of social and charitable groups representing Czechoslovaks, Jews, Hungarians, Romanians, Lithuanians, Poles, Slovenians, Serbs, Croatians, Italians and Germans. Together, these groups collaborated throughout 1945 and 1946 to reach the goal of collecting 5,000,000 pounds of clothing.[1] Groups like the Cleveland Council of Parents and Teachers, the Council of Jewish Women, the League of Women Voters, and the American Jewish Congress collected, inspected and packed the clothing for collection.

At a time when garment manufacturing companies still lined Superior Avenue and anchored neighborhoods on both sides of the Cuyahoga, some of this clothing may have been made right here in Cleveland, by immigrants who came from the very countries receiving this aid. Clevelanders collected, inspected and packed clothing for their relatives abroad. The immigrants had come full circle. Successful in America, they offered some of their bounty to Europe's most desperate refugees.

The garment industry offered significant opportunities to immigrants arriving in the United States in the late nineteenth century, helping to transform many of them into prosperous citizens. As one of the nation's centers for the production of clothing, Cleveland benefited greatly from the industry. While most of those who founded and led the firms of the garment industry were Jewish immigrants to the United States, the industry employed immigrants from eastern and southern Europe. The workforce reflected the diversity of the city and included, among other groups, Jews, Italians, Czechs, Poles, Slovenes and Hungarians. African-Americans found work in the trade, too, when they came up north in the 1910s and later in significant numbers. The industry's impact thus reached everyone in the city and region, whether they made, sold, or simply bought and wore the products being manufactured along the city's streets. Immigrants had a chance to build their lives, to feed their families, to buy homes and to establish themselves as Americans. The industry allowed the immigrants to establish lives in vibrant urban neighborhoods that continue to define the character of the city.

What can you spare that they can wear? The May Company collects clothing for war relief. (James Wattenmaker, WRHS)

Belle Did Her Bit, horse used in clothing drive, 1945. (James Wattenmaker, WRHS)

II

Paper cutting room, Joseph & Feiss, 1915. (Joseph & Feiss Company, WRHS)

Exterior of Richman Brothers store, Cleveland, 1930s. (Robert Harger, WRHS)

The rag trade or the shmate trade, more informal names for a significant industry, also affected the physical landscape and economic, social and cultural development. The factories and warehouses of the industry still line the streets of downtown. Some structures have found other purposes, while others stand like ghost towns. And, not least, the industry provided leadership to the community, as many of the founders and leaders of Cleveland's principal garment manufacturing firms took on prominent positions in the Jewish community and in the area's social service and philanthropic organizations.

By 1916, Cleveland ranked fourth nationwide in the making of women's wear and eleventh in the making of men's wear.[2] The manufacture of women's clothing was especially important in Cleveland, ranking fourth among the city's industries in 1890 and fifth in 1909.[3] Second in employment to the iron and steel industry, garment manufacturing spread through many of the city's most important neighborhoods on the East Side and the West Side. The industry in Cleveland had two important centers, in today's Warehouse District and along Superior Avenue from East 19th to East 25th Streets, but several significant firms had substantial plants farther east and south and farther west. Makers of women's wear, men's wear, children's wear, and knit goods could all be found in the city.

A key industry developed here on the banks of the Cuyahoga and then disappeared. Understanding how this happened and what this industry meant for the city teaches us about the importance of immigration, the challenges of entrepreneurship and family businesses, and the reasons for the success and failure of economic enterprise. The area's garment industry was part of what made Cleveland one of America's leading cities in the mid-twentieth century. The industry shaped the lives of those it employed and helped to define the fashions we wore at the office and at home.

What is the garment industry?

THE GARMENT INDUSTRY IS PERHAPS BEST UNDERSTOOD AS THE MANUFACTURE OF READY-TO-WEAR CLOTHING, an innovation of the modern age that not only changed what Americans wear but also how they shop and express themselves in public through choices in fashion. The garment manufacturers in the United States in the twentieth century bought their cloth from other manufacturers and, in most cases, sold their products to retailers who then sold directly to consumers. The immigrants who found themselves as owners of or workers in garment manufacturing companies were part of a long, laborious process, a process that was also subject to vicissitudes in style. The industry both shaped fashion and was subject to it.

Lloyd P. Gartner, eminent historian of American Jewry, called Isaac A. Isaacs "the balladeer of early Cleveland haberdashery." Isaacs did not make clothing, but he was one of the first in Cleveland to sell ready-made clothing. Isaacs offered his wares, retail and wholesale, at the Magnificent Union Hall Clothing Emporium, at the corner of Superior and Union. He used "The Terrifically Thrilling Poem of The Fair Inez or the Lone Lady of the Crimson Cliff, A Tale of the Sea", a story of pirates and prisoners, to advertise the Union Hall. The prisoner should have shopped at Union Hall:

> *His clothes were none of ISAACS best,*
> *He ne'er at UNION HALL had dressed;*
> *His Coat was long, his Pants quite short,*
> *He had them at some slop shop bought,*
> *For at the elbows and the knees,*
> *They had vent holes to catch the breeze.*
> *Such clothes ne'er came from UNION HALL,*
> *For ISAACS Clothes ne'er rip at all.*

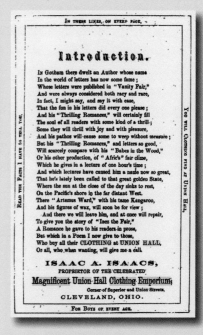

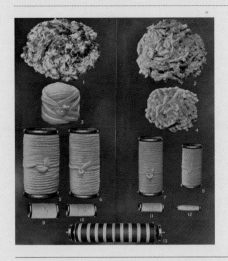

Early settlers in Ohio had to dye their own wool and make their own clothing. These are part of the instructions to dye wool blue black, from The Family Director, by Matthew Atkinson, a book published in Carrollton, Ohio, in 1844:

Five pounds of wool; boil for two hours, one peck white-oak bark, and one and a half pounds black-oak bark, ground as for tanning, then take out the bark, and dissolve three-fourths of a pound copperas and two ounces blue vitriol, and add to the dye, stir well and dip the wool, and boil slowly one hour... From wool to cloth. (Michael and Rosemary Hritsko and Bruce Gifford, WRHS)

Before any garment can be produced, fiber must be turned into material that can be used for clothing. The coat of sheep or goats must be spun into yarn. Cotton must be woven into cloth. Because we want to wear clothes that are red, blue or green and often brightly patterned, the producers of cloth and yarn must dye their product before the manufacturer can turn it into a sweater, dress, cloak, suit or other garment. Knitting mills turn yarn from suppliers into clothing; cut and sew firms cut the cloth according to various patterns and then assemble that cloth into clothes. The complex process of putting together an item of clothing involves designing the garment to be produced; acquiring the raw material to make the garment; measuring, sponging (shrinking) and testing the cloth that has been purchased for the making of the garment; grading and marking the pattern; cutting the cloth; sewing the garment; and pressing and examining the product. Knitting mills, working with yarn, not cloth, follow the same steps but with some variation. The yarn used must be dyed and tested before workers operating various machines that enable a wide array of color and pattern combinations can turn it into clothing. Workers had to cut the cloth carefully, and the yarn had to be strong and the colors fast. If not, there was waste, which cost the company, and, ultimately, the employee.

Flat machines used for trim and collars, Frisch Knitting Mills, 1950s. (Marc Frisch, WRHS)

Clothing factories employ many more than those involved directly in these tasks. Others help to plan production and operations. Still more work in the mechanical department, overseeing and repairing the machines, or in packing and shipping. Some factories, depending on the garments they produce, may also embroider, pleat and tuck, though separate companies are sometimes hired to perform these tasks. The clothing factory is only an intermediary step between the origins of the fabric and the shirt on someone's back. The final steps are delivery to the retail store and sale to the consumer.

The industry is dependent on the market, which changes its taste according to fashion. Fashion creates the need for flexibility and introduces significant complexity into the industry. Firms must be

Today we all wear ready-to-wear clothing. Most of us think of custom made clothing as a luxury, if we even realize that it is possible to buy clothing that is custom fit. But in the early nineteenth century, before technological advances made the mass production of clothing possible, all clothing was custom made. A cutter at Richman Brothers shows how cloth was cut for mass production. **Cutting room, Richman Brothers, ca. 1930s.** (Robert Harger, WRHS)

WHERE WAS CLEVELAND'S GARMENT DISTRICT?

Two neighborhoods can make a strong claim to being Cleveland's garment district. The first is known today as the Warehouse District, especially the area bounded by Lakeside and Superior on the north and south and West 3rd Street and West 9th Street on the east and west. This was close to Public Square and one of the first areas to be settled by residents and shopkeepers. Joseph & Feiss, Printz-Biederman, L.N. Gross and many others were located in this neighborhood.

Another neighborhood with a claim to the title lies farther east along Superior, between East 19th Street and East 30th Street. H. Black and John Anisfield were two of the first companies to locate here. Others followed, including Lampl Fashions and S. Korach Co. The construction of I-90 cut through the middle of the neighborhood. Today a row of factory and warehouse buildings stands as testament to the area's industrial past from East 19th Street to East 25th Street.

So many companies lay outside of these neighborhoods, however, that it may be best to give up the idea of one neighborhood known as the garment district. East 55th Street just south of Superior Avenue

was the site of Richman Brothers. Many of that company's employees came from the surrounding neighborhood, populated mostly by Slovenians. Joseph & Feiss eventually located on the West Side, on West 53rd Street, just south of Lorain (and now south of I-90). Still other companies, like Kaynee and Cleveland Worsted Mills, were located southeast of downtown, in what is today known as Slavic Village. Buckeye Garment Rental, a part of Work Wear, was located on East 93rd Street, close to today's Union-Miles neighborhood.

Cleveland's once efficient public transportation system easily funneled workers from one neighborhood to another, so the residential pattern of workers in the industry was diffuse as well. Some lived near the companies where they worked, while others went downtown from other city neighborhoods. Late in the twentieth century some companies moved even farther away from the city. Dalton set up shop in Willoughby, and L.N. Gross and Euclid Garment Manufacturing had plants in Kent. **Map from L. N. Gross scrapbook.** (Louis N. Gross and Elaine D. Gross, WRHS)

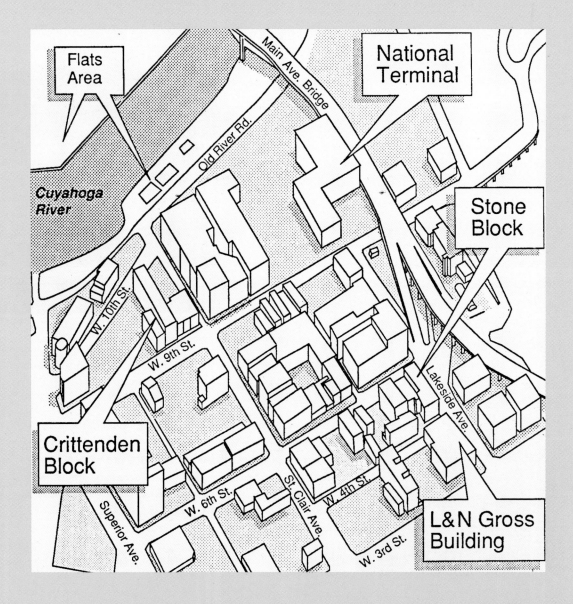

ready to change production methods as new kinds of garments are introduced. This means using various designs, ordering different kinds of machines and training workers to handle the changes in the garments being produced. Mass production was indeed profitable, but the demands of making a variety of garments often made it difficult for entrepreneurs to be successful. The garment industry never offered a quick profit. For those immigrants who became involved in the industry, though, it did offer an opportunity. Those who succeeded were the most flexible in their thinking, ready to take risks, to change to other products, and to stem costs during an economic downturn.

Folding and stacking room, Joseph & Feiss, ca. 1930s. (Joseph & Feiss Company, WRHS)

The industry had its roots in the production of clothing in private homes and then in small shops and underwent tremendous change from 1750 to 1850. This change involved both the mechanization and organization of labor, as workers moved from producing homespun goods to clothing made of imported fabrics. The technological innovations of the mid-nineteenth century, and those that followed, made possible almost limitless choices in fashion for men, women and children. In 1846, Elias Howe was granted a patent for the sewing machine, which enabled a transition from handwork to manufacturing on a much greater scale. War, too, played a role in the mechanization of the garment industry. The needs of the military during the Civil War spurred production and mechanization, allowing the ready-to-wear segment of the industry to grow exponentially. Changes in population growth, technology and communications meant more people to clothe, more rapid changes in fashion, more diversity in style and product and more international cooperation and competition.

The growth of ready-to-wear changed the way people lived. When people could buy clothing in shops at affordable prices, there was less need to learn how to make these garments at home. That meant fewer women learning how to sew. The transition to ready-to-wear over the course of the late nineteenth and early twentieth centuries necessitated the growth of the industry. The garment industry helped to make us modern, providing much needed economic opportunities and offering the clothing and goods needed for personal and professional success.

The industry prospered in Cleveland during the period of greatest immigration, from the 1880s to the 1920s and then surged again after World War II. The decline of the industry coincided with industrial decline in other areas. American manufacturers closed for a number of reasons, not least including foreign competition and, to a lesser extent, conflicts between management and labor. As early as the 1940s, garment manufacturers relocated their enterprises to the American South and overseas

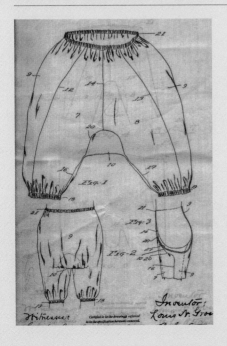

Cleveland Heights resident Louis N. Gross received a patent in 1932 for an apparatus for piling layers of fabric. Cutters cut through piles of fabric. This patent referred to an improved method of piling the fabric that minimized wrinkling. Gross also applied for other patents, some of which concerned the seams, stitching and elasticity of bloomer garments. Drawing in patent for construction of crotch seams in bloomers. (Louis N. Gross and Elaine D. Gross, WRHS)

in response to the rising cost of labor and the need for flexibility. The industry ceased to be an active sector of the city's economy long ago. The late twentieth century transformations and closures of the area's garment manufacturers affected the city as much as the growth of the industry spurred economic development and neighborhood growth. Job losses led workers to leave neighborhoods in the city for more opportunities in the suburbs or out of state. Just as the losses of the region's larger steel and oil industries affected daily life, so, too, did the loss of the garment industry. The virtual disappearance of a once vibrant sector of the economy handed the region's leaders yet more challenges. How should we help manufacturers and employees transition to new fields? What do we do with once bustling, now empty factories?

"The fall season is just beginning…", Yiddish language advertisement for Richman Bros. Company at Ontario and Prospect, in *Di yidishe velt*, September 10, 1913.

The history of the garment industry has long been a topic of great interest to Cleveland's Jewish community. Community leaders expressed their interest in learning more about the industry as early as the 1980s, when they cooperated closely with Western Reserve Historical Society to collect materials from firms and individuals. Stanley Garfinkel, a professor of history at Kent State University, conducted a series of oral history interviews over a number of years in the early 1980s. Such activities reveal the extent of the community's interest and are themselves indicators of the significance of the industry for the community. Many in the community still have memories of working in the industry in the 1950s and 1960s, sometimes even earlier.

In spite of such enthusiastic interest, however, sources for this history are not easy to find. As the late Judah Rubinstein, the city's foremost chronicler of the community's Jewish history, put it, "Looking for written records? Forget it!"[4] For whatever reasons, the records of many of the most significant companies in the industry have not been preserved. Those that were reveal a growing city that has undergone remarkable transformations in the last hundred years. Most of the smaller firms are not represented in archival collections at all, while some larger firms left behind only a few boxes of materials.

Unfortunately, relatively few garments from Cleveland's many garment manufacturing firms have been preserved. The holdings of WRHS related to fashion and the garment industry have received national recognition, as evidenced by their inclusion in a 2005 exhibit on American Jews and the gar-

Jerry Frisch of The H.E. Frisch Knitting Mills Company explained the difficulties of the industry in a talk at John Carroll University in 1967:

Our mills must 'tool up' 4-5 times a year. When I say tool up, I mean to create a new line for each season. Sometimes we must even plan more than the seasonal lines to bring out new looks during and between seasons. When planning a new line, many factors must be taken into consideration. In addition to style, which of course is all-important, new colors must be contemplated, new and different types of yarn must be taken into consideration and above all, new and different types of stitches must be created on our versatile knitting machinery. Often new machinery is required to keep abreast of the market for cost-savings, individuality and originality. Changes must be done fast so a season won't be lost and it is not uncommon to switch from natural fibers to synthetic and vice versa, or switch from ladies' to men's to children's items from one season to another. Because of the innate nature of the style business, we must at all times be on our toes for the demands of the consumer who after all is the greatest style creator of all. Jacquard knitting machines, Frisch Knitting Mills, 1950s. (Marc Frisch, WRHS)

A formidable row of buildings lines Superior Avenue between 19th and 25th Streets. These buildings housed some of the most well-known names in the industry, including Black and Lampl. What were they like inside? A description of the Korach Building at 2400 Superior Ave., built in 1912 and designed by the well-known firm Walker and Weeks, tells us.

The offices and showrooms were lined with oak panels. Hardwood floors and terrazzo tile completed the impression of office efficiency. Shipping was located on the east side of the first floor and manufacturing on the west side. The second floor housed the cutting room, manufacturing area and pressing departments. Piece goods sponging, warehousing and other tasks were located in the basement, along with the employee cafeteria. After the Korach family closed their company in the 1930s, Weinberger Drug Co. (later Gray Drug) leased the building. The Gray Drug lease with the Korach family ended in 1977. The S. H. Hexter Co. then converted the entire building to warehousing. In 2014 the building was home to an art gallery and Hotcards, a printing firm. The S. Korach Co. building at 2400 Superior Avenue. (Jeff Korach, WRHS)

ment industry at Yeshiva University Museum.[5] But while these garments help us tell the story of Jews in the garment industry in the United States, they are not directly related to Cleveland. In addition, the clothing manufactured here was usually more utilitarian than high fashion, intended for a middle-class market. The dresses, blouses, sweaters, cloaks and suits were worn and worn out. Such materials are not often saved for posterity, and relatively few examples are preserved in costume collections.

This study outlines the history of the industry in an effort to understand how manufacturers influenced the industry, the development of the city, and the growth of the Jewish community. Materials examined for this study include the manuscript collections and picture groups held at WRHS, published studies of the garment industry and publications related specifically to the firms established in Cleveland, and materials from other local institutions, including the Cleveland Public Library and Kent State University. These materials include oral histories, taken by participants in WRHS projects from the 1980s to 2000s. These oral histories, with owners and employees and their descendants, offer diverse perspectives of the challenges and opportunities the industry provided. Those interested in the city's economy and the history of labor will want to explore many questions about the industry and its influence in much more significant detail than that offered here. There is still much to learn about the demographics of the workforce, the views of workers and the role of technological innovation in the industry, among other topics. In addition, the industry in the city should be compared directly with other industries and with garment manufacturing elsewhere. This study presents the industry as it developed in Cleveland and is based primarily on sources in the Library and Archives at Western Reserve Historical Society.

Edith Anisfield, the daughter of garment manufacturer John Anisfield, established the Anisfield-Book Awards in 1935, naming them after her father and her husband, Eugene Wolf. She used her family's estate to further her passion for social justice. The Anisfield-Wolf Book Awards honor titles that examine issues of racism and diversity. Nobel Prize winners such as Martin Luther King, Jr., Nadine Gordimer and Toni Morrison have been recognized for their work. King was recognized for Stride toward Freedom: The Montgomery Story in 1959; Nadine Gordimer for her novel, A Sport of Nature in 1988; and Toni Morrison for Beloved, also in 1988.

The Anisfield-Wolf Book Awards

Opening Minds. Challenging Minds.™

The Anisfield-Wolf Book Awards, honoring titles that examine racism and diversity, were established by Edith Anisfield Wolf, the daughter of John Anisfield.

From the dry goods stores of the 1840s to the factories and international operations of the 1980s, the garment industry has been of great importance to the area's Jewish community and to the city more generally. The most prominent characters in the story are the owners of the factories. They are more visible, though not necessarily of greater importance, than the thousands of workers who knitted and sewed their way to the American dream. Their wealth gave them a status in the community workers could not attain easily. They also sometimes left behind records in the wake of their companies. Men like Moritz Joseph, Kaufman Hays, Samuel Rosenthal and Maurice Saltzman were the leaders of an industry that came to be associated with the Jewish community even as this industry affected nearly all the residents of the city.

Richman Brothers, undated.
(Robert Harger, WRHS)

Advertisement for rayon fabric.
(Robert J. Kahn, WRHS)

Hundreds of firms in the industry came and went from the 1840s on. Those discussed here are the ones we know most about. Generalizations are dangerous. Each family firm found its own niche in the market. The families and the firms they created often merged, personally and professionally. The story of this community, then, includes the personal motivations of individuals – their strengths and weaknesses – and the demands of business, and of workers at every stage in the process of making a garment. The focus here is specifically on the manufacture of garments and not on the retail sector of the industry, a topic worthy of much further study on its own. Manufacturers certainly interacted with retailers in order to sell their products, and connections between manufacturers and retailers were often quite important to those working in the industry. Retailers such as the May Co., Higbee Co., Halle Brothers Co. and Jo-Ann Fabrics have storied pasts of their own and deserve separate treatment, apart from the histories of the companies discussed here.

The arc of the industry's story is clear, reaching upwards until the late twentieth century, at least until the 1970s, and then turning sharply downward as manufacturers left the market from the 1960s to the 1990s. The success of the industry cannot be said to have been fleeting, but it was temporary. Garment manufacturers fell victim to the same market forces that propelled the entrance of their ancestors into the industry. Workers wanted higher wages. Labor abroad was cheaper. The government did not protect the industry, and so free trade meant the collapse of most of the last apparel firms in the United States in the early twenty-first century.

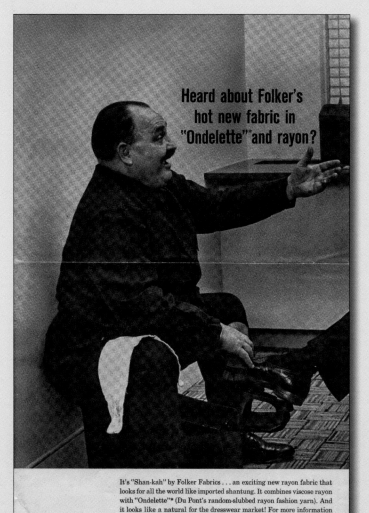

Heard about Folker's hot new fabric in "Ondelette"* and rayon?

It's "Shan-kah" by Folker Fabrics . . . an exciting new rayon fabric that looks for all the world like imported shantung. It combines viscose rayon with "Ondelette"* (Du Pont's random-slubbed rayon fashion yarn). And it looks like a natural for the dresswear market! For more information

Enjoy "The Du Pont Show With June Allyson", Monday Nights—10:30 E.S.T.—CBS-TV.
*Remember: "Ondelette" is Du Pont's new trademark for the random-slubbed rayon fashion yarn formerly known as Ondulé.

Two themes stand out in the long period of the industry's success, the entrepreneurship of the immigrant and the conflict between management and labor. The immigrant's willingness (and need) to take risks sometimes, but not always, paid off. The workers' struggle for better conditions and higher wages concerns the very nature of the entrepreneur's task. Cleveland had its share of entrepreneurs and its share of labor conflict. This conflict, not always resolved easily, was part of the struggle of the immigrant, whether manufacturer or worker, to succeed. The garment industry in Cleveland was a vehicle for the Americanization of both manufacturer and worker. The industry, in which Jewish immigrants played the most substantial role, enabled the success of other immigrants and contributed to the growth of Cleveland as a center of manufacturing.

The industry's success in the city made so much possible for so many – clothes, homes and consumer goods. If the streets here were not magically paved with gold, they nonetheless were lined with shops and factories that needed immigrant labor and offered a leg up after a tumultuous journey from Europe. The garment industry enabled the community to sustain itself and then to grow exponentially, in terms of wealth and influence. Because their ancestors made clothing for a living, the sons and daughters of the entrepreneurs could become teachers, doctors, lawyers or anything else they desired. The industry offered them the opportunity to make choices of their own, not choices out of necessity. The most successful developed into important philanthropists. The shmates they sold turned into hospitals, schools, and art and cultural centers.

The following chapters trace the history of the industry from its beginnings to its decline. The period of early immigration saw changes in the industry as a result of technology and the demands of soldiers during the Civil War. The influx of immigrants from the 1880s on helped to change the industry significantly, as factories developed and manufacturers began to participate fully in Cleveland's civic life. World Wars I and II brought significant change to an industry, asking manufacturers to retool their operations to meet national demands. In the postwar period, the industry both contributed to and benefited from the general peacetime prosperity. Finally, a review of the decline of the industry helps us understand how the city changed over the course of the late twentieth century.

score better than ever with *Hadley*

It's profit time for all Pros! Start now offering your customers the finest designer coordinates fashioned for perfect fit and comfort. Remember! The better your customers look, the better the pay-off for you. For additional information, contact Hadley-Active, Dalton Blvd., Willoughby, Ohio 44094. Hadley – a division of Dalton

women's and men's apparel

Advertisement for Hadley sportswear, 1970s.
(Arthur, Ken, Jim, and Bob Dery, WRHS)

DALTON. FASHION PORT OF THE WORLD.

CRUISE INTO SPRING

Dalton
James Kenrob
Robert Arthur

Dalton sales book, 1980.
(Arthur, Ken, Jim, and Bob Dery, WRHS)

"*Like a very large*

overgrown village"

ISAAC JOSEPH, ONE OF THE FIRST OF THE JOSEPH FAMILY MEMBERS TO BE INVOLVED WITH THE GARMENT INDUSTRY, came to Cleveland to work as a bookkeeper in 1873, for the firm then known as Koch & Loeb. He recalled his first days in Cleveland in 1923. Joseph wrote that the city was "like a very large overgrown village".[1] He was impressed with the splendor of Euclid Avenue, then lined with the mansions that would earn the street the nickname Millionaires' Row. Nonetheless, Joseph described the business section as "rather mean and dingy". Over the decades, Joseph and his family helped to turn Koch & Loeb into Joseph & Feiss, contributing to the growth of Cleveland's business district and helping to transform the city into a place that would eventually be known as the best location in the nation.

Richman's, near East 8th Street and Euclid Avenue in downtown Cleveland, early twentieth century.
(Penny Wightman Dalzell, WRHS)

Jews and the Garment Industry

L IKE THE RESIDENTS OF THE CITY, THE GARMENT INDUSTRY CAME TO CLEVELAND FROM SOMEWHERE ELSE and maintained close ties with relatives in other cities. The growing city of Cleveland increasingly attracted new businesses and immigrants throughout the mid-nineteenth century. Joseph & Feiss, the city's largest and arguably most well-known manufacturer, began as a store in Meadville, Pennsylvania, in 1841, relocating to Cleveland's Superior Street in 1845. Another of Cleveland's well-known companies, Richman Brothers, also had its start outside the city, in Portsmouth, a town on the Ohio River directly south of Columbus, in 1853. The company came to Cleveland's West 9th Street in 1879. Several manufacturers, such as L.N. Gross, got their start in New York before moving to a regional center like Cleveland for better opportunities.

Cleveland's garment manufacturers provided a range of products for their customers throughout the country: cloaks, dresses and cashmere sweaters for women, among other garments, and shirts, trousers and business suits for men. An important segment of the industry in the city manufactured uniforms for workers and soldiers. The city also hosted the firms that supplied the manufacturers with the items they needed, whether dye for cloth, buttons, or boxes and packaging. Between the 1890s and 1940s 7 percent of Cleveland's working population was employed in the garment industry.[2] Firms such as Joseph & Feiss, Richman Brothers, Printz-Biederman, Lion Knitting Mills and Lampl Fashions were well-known by consumers before World War II. Postwar growth added a few other names to the roster of successful firms in Cleveland, including Ohio Knitting Mills, Bobbie Brooks and Dalton.

But the importance of making clothing for the Jewish community is difficult to overestimate. Among the most economically desperate of immigrant populations, Jews entered the industry at a propitious time, when ready-to-wear clothing was taking off and increasing numbers of women could afford new fashions.[3] It is possible to attribute the economic success of Jewish immigrants before World War I not just to the garment industry generally, but more specifically to the growth in demand for fashionable women's and men's wear.[4] In 1900, a third of all Jews in the workforce in the United

Superior at Public Square, 1880s. (WRHS)

States were employed in the manufacture of garments.[5] Those already established in the business also benefited from the decrease in immigration during and after World War I. Fewer immigrants meant less competition, and so businesses could grow under favorable conditions that ultimately helped to contribute to the economic success of the American Jewish community.[6] American Jewish entrepreneurs simply had good timing.[7]

Why did Jews work in the garment industry? The answer may be as simple as the explanation offered by Louis N. Gross in his memoir. Writing of his brother and other family members, Gross explained, "the type of work that they found convenient to obtain and learn was the garment business."

Why Waste Your Time?

You might as well come to us direct, if you're looking for the best clothes your money can buy. You'll save time and money.

Where else can you find guaranteed pure wool, stylish, well-made clothes retailing from $10 to $25.

CLOTHCRAFT CLOTHES embody all these qualities.

The Goldsmith Joseph Feiss Co.
Cleveland, Ohio.

The Cleveland Trade Bulletin, 1905.

Ken Dery offered a similar explanation for the involvement of his father, the Hungarian Jewish immigrant Arthur Dery, in the garment business.[8] Arthur Dery, a generation younger than Louis N. Gross, entered the business because, according to his son, "he needed to eat."[9] Once factories were up and running, the industry offered even greater opportunities. Armin Guggenheim's father, a refugee from Germany who arrived in Cleveland in 1939, first found work in a local factory sweeping floors.[10] Still later, the industry offered opportunities to Hungarian refugees in 1956, such as Agnes Harichovszky, who found work at Ohio Knitting Mills and eventually became one of the firm's most valued employees.[11]

People got into the business because they thought they could make money. Whether homemade or manufactured, the tedious nature of the work and our desire for different, better clothing to wear have always made producing garments a particularly challenging task. Yet for the immigrant with few other options, it was a short step from selling fabric to making and selling garments of all kinds. The industry offered few barriers to entry and so became the place many immigrants started. The workshops and factories offered immigrants a comfortable environment, physically and socially. Other workers spoke their language and many shops were closed on Saturday, allowing them to maintain religious traditions. Many lived close to the factory as well.[12]

An Industry Develops

CLEVELAND WAS A SMALL TOWN UNTIL THE OHIO AND ERIE CANAL SPURRED THE GROWTH OF THE CITY IN THE 1820s and determined its development as a center for trade. Cleveland's location as the terminus of the Ohio and Erie Canal helped shape the course of the region's development. The city offered farmers a more effective means of distribution, and its location assured that it would become a manufacturing center. The production of ready-to-wear clothing had already begun when Cleveland started to grow in the 1820s and when Cleveland's first Jewish immigrants came to the city in 1839.

The Cleveland Trade Bulletin, 1905.

The region's growth in the first decades of the nineteenth century attracted such men as Simpson Thorman, a trader in hides from Unsleben, Bavaria, and the first permanent Jewish settler. In a classic example of the chain migration that would continue among the Jewish community, Thorman reached back to Europe and brought over his family and friends to settle in this growing frontier town. When they arrived, Cleveland had just started to grow. Jews were among the region's early immigrant groups. They joined the Irish who had come to build the canals and the Germans who had fled increasingly difficult political and economic circumstances. Four woolen mills were operating in the Cleveland area in 1840.[13] The city directory for 1846-1847 listed 19 drapers and tailors, 14 dressmakers, and 5 tailoresses.[14] Most clothes were still made at home, but technological innovations associated with the sewing machine would soon encourage mass production and the growth of a number of firms making and selling clothing. The federal census of 1860 listed 29 principal industrial classifications in Cuyahoga County. With 27 firms employing nearly a thousand men and women, clothing was second only to lumber as the region's most important economic activity.[15] But the manufacture of garments would never become the center of the region's economy.

Cleveland was in the forefront of technological development. The middle decades of the nineteenth century saw tremendous growth in the iron and steel industry. Workers in the industry, many of them Welsh immigrants, processed the iron and steel into the parts needed in the production of the era's new machines. John D. Rockefeller turned the city into an important oil refinery center in the 1860s, cementing Cleveland's reputation as a promising industrial powerhouse. More than any other economic activity, Cleveland's heavy industry defined the city by attracting the immigrants who would build the neighborhoods and churches that clustered near the mills and smokestacks.

Benjamin Franklin Peixotto, one of Cleveland's earliest Jewish settlers, helped to establish one of the first successful garment manufacturing firms in the city. Peixotto had come to Cleveland in 1836 at the age of 2; his father Daniel was the first Jewish doctor to teach medicine in Ohio, at Willoughby Medical College. The Peixotto family left the area in 1841, but Benjamin Franklin Peixotto returned as a young man to become an important leader in the community. He eventually entered

Just as owners of garment manufacturing firms brought over their families to work in the industry, so, too, did workers recommend their family members, friends, and acquaintances for work. Printz-Biederman offered its employees financial incentives if a recommended employee worked at least six weeks. They offered more for experienced applicants and offered special seasonal prizes for those who recommended the largest number of applicants. Coat department, sewing floor of Joseph & Feiss. (Joseph & Feiss Company, WRHS)

Advertisement for Davis, Peixotto & Co., early 1860s. (WRHS)

into business with George A. Davis, a Jewish immigrant from Germany who was selling ready made clothing in a shop he opened in 1847. Davis, Peixotto & Co. manufactured thousands of uniforms for the Union during the Civil War.[16] The years of the Civil War were good for the firm, and the garment industry. The need to clothe so many men led to increased standardization in measurements, which enabled manufacturers to produce their goods more efficiently. The firm closed not long after the war, in 1867.

Seamstress at Joseph & Feiss demonstrating bad posture for study of employees' work habits, 1923. (Joseph & Feiss, WRHS)

While both Peixotto and Davis eventually left for New York, the story of their company reveals a familiar pattern seen in the garment industry in later decades. Jewish immigrants established a successful enterprise, became leading philanthropists in the community, and aided their newly adopted country during a period of war. Peixotto and Davis founded the Hebrew Benevolent Society in 1855, less than twenty years after the Jewish community had gotten its start in Cleveland with the arrival of the immigrants from Unsleben. Peixotto, active in B'nai B'rith and a former president of Cleveland's Mercantile Library Association and Young Men's Hebrew Literary Society, went on to become American consul to Romania in 1870.

Another Jewish immigrant from Germany, Joseph Hays, described the link between peddling and the garment industry in his autobiography. Having arrived in the 1850s, after a few of his many siblings had already set up in Cleveland, he was given items by his family members to peddle in the small towns and settlements east of Cleveland. Hays describes going door to door in what is now Shaker Heights and Gates Mills, trudging down paths and past bushes, to meet families who needed the goods he had for sale.[17] From peddling, many immigrants then were able to develop their own stores. They often produced what they sold. While not all those who peddled became independent storeowners or manufacturers, many did turn to the production of clothing because it was something that could be made easily in the home. In addition, some immigrants had experience in this kind of craft back home in Europe.

Kaufman Hays, one of Joseph's siblings who arrived in the States before he did, offers us an example of how an innovation encouraged sales and helped the industry grow. Kaufman Hays worked in several different stores as a young man, buying and selling the goods that were making their way to this growing industrial city. When Kaufman Hays worked at the City Mills Store in the late 1850s, he discovered a large pile of calico, purple with white dots. The ends were all faded. He cut the fabric into pieces and sold the remnants. The women who frequented the store soon developed the habit of coming in to the store to look for more, and the firm made sure Hays always had remnants to sell.[18] Hays' action illustrates the creative reuse of materials, a hallmark of the garment industry and an example of the industry's low barriers to entry.[19]

At the same time that Kaufman Hays was selling remnants and Davis and Peixotto were making ready-to-wear clothes, Joseph & Feiss and Richman Brothers, two of the biggest names in the history of the industry in Cleveland, were just getting their start. These firms were two of the area's oldest and best-known garment manufacturing companies, and their histories illustrate how the garment industry developed, prospered, and then became an integral part of the city's economic fabric. Koch & Loeb, a wholesale clothing store selling men's clothes and piece goods, was founded in Meadville, Pennsylvania, in 1841, and relocated to Cleveland in 1845. Koch & Loeb also manufactured its own brand of clothing, but it contracted the work out to small ethnic shops, themselves examples of the differentiation of an ethnic niche economy. Bohemians (Czechs) operated coat and overcoat shops; the Germans made pants, later known as trousers. Hungarians and Germans made vests.[20]

Koch & Loeb changed its name several times throughout the decades as partners came and went. Moritz Joseph became involved with the firm in the 1860s, when he still lived in New York and the company set up a short-lived branch there. He eventually decided to move to Cleveland with his family. His son Isaac Joseph arrived in 1873 to take the position of bookkeeper for the firm. Julius Feiss,

From The Loop, published by The Kaynee Co., March 1916:

White blouses and Easter go hand in hand. Easter is the one day when nearly every mother puts a white blouse on Bill.

The Kaynee White Blouse display is unusual. The styles are purchase-compelling, and our white blouses are guaranteed fast color. This may sound like a joke, but it isn't.

The marked shortage of bleach has forced many makers to use white materials improperly prepared, and they turn yellow when washed. Kaynee white goods will remain always absolutely the same pure white.

The Dollar Blouse is the blouse to show. Laundered with and without plaits, and unlaundered with full French cuffs.

Everything you have a call for blouses before Easter, make the white blouse suggestion, and INCREASE YOUR EASTER SALES

Kaufman Hays, early Jewish settler who peddled calico remnants and later became one of the city's most significant leaders in the late nineteenth century. (Michael Louis Hays, WRHS)

Joseph & Feiss Co. at West 53rd Street between Train Avenue and Walworth Avenue, ca. 1920. (Joseph & Feiss Company, WRHS)

whose sons Paul and Richard would play important roles in the development of the business, started at the company in the 1870s as well.

Koch & Loeb, later Joseph & Feiss, can serve as an example of the way the industry usually worked. The manufacturer purchased the raw materials, determined the product to be made, farmed the work out to independent contractors (usually immigrant women working in their homes), and then sold the product to retailers or directly to the consumer. The selling of the product often involved traveling salesmen, even as early as the mid-nineteenth century. The manufacturer was usually not directly involved in the production of the cloth, nor did the manufacturer actually make the product. The contractors, some of them with skills they brought from Europe, made the product. The cutting, trimming, sewing, and finishing of the product took place offsite.[21] Because manufacturers used so many different contractors, there was no way to guarantee uniformity in the finished product; each contractor would turn out something slightly different.

The firm grew significantly in the 1870s, when it sent out five or six traveling salesmen throughout Ohio, Indiana, Michigan, and western Pennsylvania. The salesmen carried with them sample garments in heavy trunks, showing retailers alpaca coats, vests, seersucker suits, and overcoats. By the mid-1870s the company installed cutting machines, marking a significant improvement in quality and uniformity. The firm that eventually became known as

Several companies held events for their employees at Euclid Beach Park, one of the area's most popular amusement parks. (WRHS)

EUCLID BEACH

Printzess
Suit No. 104

What more charming could any woman desire than this chic and smartly designed suit? Sides are belted and the fur trimmed pockets end in a loose plait at the side back, where a bit of Hercules braid is effectively used. The collar of Hudson Seal is made in convertible fashion. This clever model will be appreciated by the woman who is on the lookout for a "different" or unusual style.

Material: Beautiful quality, All-wool Duvet de Laine.
Lining: Peau de Cygne Silk.
Colors: Navy, Taupe, Brown or Prunella.

Advertisement, Printz-Biederman Company. (Judah Rubinstein, WRHS)

Owners cared about the education of their employees because this knowledge affected the bottom line. Work in the garment industry was also very specialized. A committee at Printz-Biederman met to determine guidelines for the education of assistants and came up with the following guidelines:

First: That they should know the colors of cloth.

Second: They are to know the names of the different cloths, linings and trimmings.

Third: They are to know garment style numbers and their names.

Fourth: That the head of the stock keeping department, show and teach those working with him, how to hang up garments properly, special attention to be given to plush garments and the proper way to carry garments.

Fifth: To explain to them the responsibility and inter-relationship between the customer, their work and this institution

Sixth: Mr. J. R. Printz to direct the teaching of matters relative to cloths.

Seventh: That a meeting for these instructions be held once every week, preferably on Monday morning between 10:30 and 11:00 o'clock.

Joseph & Feiss developed an internal manufacturing operation in 1897.

Richman Brothers, one of Joseph & Feiss' local competitors in men's wear, had a similar start. Founded in 1853 by Henry Richman, Sr., in Portsmouth, Ohio, the Henry Richman Company originally operated as many who started in the garment industry did, by cutting cloth that was then sent in horse-drawn carts to contractors to finish. The final products were then sold wholesale. The family and company moved to Cleveland's Water Street (West 9th) in 1879. The founder's sons, Nathan, Charles, and Henry, took over in 1904 and the firm became Richman Brothers. Unlike other garment manufacturing companies, Richman Brothers would eventually become known for selling directly to consumers through their own retail outlets. The company prospered by offering their suits at wholesale prices, initially at $10, then at $22.50 in the 1920s and 1930s and at $49.95 in 1968. Traveling salesmen sold shirts in hotel lobbies and catalogs sold the suits through mail order. The company then set up its own retail stores to sell its products, making it the only sizable garment manufacturing company in Cleveland to sell directly to customers. In 1906 the first stores were opened in Cincinnati and Cleveland, and the business grew.

The 1870s also saw the establishment of a number of other firms. Notably, their proprietors were some of the first Jewish immigrants from Eastern Europe. David Black, the city's first Jewish immigrant from Hungary, arrived in the 1850s and began making cloaks for women in 1854.[22] He left the city in 1894, when his designer Moritz Printz entered a partnership with Joseph Biederman to form the Printz-Biederman Co. Another Jewish immigrant from Hungary, Jacob Landesman, arrived the same year David Black began making cloaks. Landesman became a traveling salesman for a cloak and ladies dress firm shortly after he arrived and then started his own business with A. W. Sampliner in 1878. The Landesman firm eventually became known as the Landesman-Hirschheimer Cloak Co. In 1870 brothers Simon and David Rosenblatt started the firm eventually known as Euclid Garment Manufacturing Co.[23] John Anisfield, a graduate of Kraków's Jagiellonian University, arrived in Cleveland in 1876 and found work at the D. Black Cloak Company. Anisfield worked there for six years before starting his own company, the John Anisfield Company, located at Superior and 22nd Street.

Like Peixotto and Davis, these men, too, took on prominent positions in the community, reflective of their commercial success, their ties with each other, and their com-

Henry Richman, Sr., 1890s. (Robert Harger, WRHS)

Stadium Clock at Cleveland Arena, advertising Richman Brothers, 1930s. (Robert Harger, WRHS)

SEWING MACHINES

Who invented the sewing machine? It's not an easy question to answer. Some say Elias Howe. Others give credit to a Frenchman, Barthélemy Thimmonier, or to the American innovater and entrepreneur Isaac Singer. Whatever the merits of their claims, the complex machine used to make clothing transformed our world. The machine improved the lives of those making clothing at home and enabled the growth of the garment industry. The machines that were later built for use in large factories performed many of the same operations as the sewing machines in people's homes.

Since men's clothing was easier to make in factories than women's clothing, women's ready-to-wear developed much later than men's. As a result, people needed sewing machines at home to continue to make clothing, even after the garment industry had taken off in the late nineteenth century. Sewing machines also enabled individuals and families to establish workshops in homes.

Singer sewing machines were sold in Cleveland as early as the 1860s. Isaac A. Isaacs, Cleveland's self-styled "clothier-poet", sold the machines at his Union Hall warehouse. Singer may be the best-known brand name, but one Cleveland firm established a brand that led to startling international success. Thomas H. White moved his White Manufacturing Company from Massachusetts to Cleveland in 1866. Ten years later his successful enterprise was known as The White Sewing Machine Company. White's sons branched out and formed the White Motor Corporation in 1906, but the White Sewing Machine Company continued its success producing sewing machines. The company flourished in the mid-twentieth century, renaming itself White Consolidated Industries to reflect its increasing diversification in other kinds of appliances. Sales increased from $1.2 billion in 1975 to $2 billion in 1985. AB Electrolux of Sweden acquired the company in 1986 and continues to operate.

While The White Sewing Machine Company did not manufacture garments, the firm's products allowed for the growth of the field. The production of the machines used in the garment industry is itself an important topic and one that was often crucial to the success of garment industry entrepreneurs. Technological innovations often meant that new product lines could be introduced, which meant more sales opportunities, and, hence, more profit. Combining parts of a suit, ca. 1930s. (Joseph & Feiss Company, WRHS)

White Sewing Machine Company, 1870s. (WRHS)

mitment to the Jewish community and to charity. For example, Jacob Landesman served as president of at least three different organizations, Mt. Sinai Hospital, the Infants' Orphan Home, and the Hungarian Aid Society. John Anisfield, too, served as president of Mt. Sinai Hospital and the Infants' Orphan Home. He also established Camp Anisfield, a camp for Jewish working girls presented to the Jewish Business Girls' Vacation Club.

As the industry grew, working conditions sometimes drew the notice of outsiders. When Susan B. Anthony visited Cleveland in the 1870s and noticed the poor working conditions in the workshops and factories, she promptly decided to advertise Thomas H. White's sewing machines alongside the cause of suffrage.[24] Anthony recognized that technological innovations could change the face of the industry and help with her explicitly political cause. Over the years, both owners and workers would use their connections to individuals and movements outside of Cleveland to help improve their own positions back home. After just a few decades of growth in the industry, some trends were becoming clear. This complex industry involving the work of many individuals in the completion of a single garment held tremendous growth potential. Workers themselves were increasingly empowered, through aid from their employers, outsiders like Anthony, and, not least, their own initiative, to improve their circumstances.

Shrinking fabric, Richman Brothers, 1930s. (Robert Harger, WRHS)

Richman Brothers, Ontario, Ohio, 1930s.
(Robert Harger, WRHS)

2 | Industry and Immigrants

"When 'the man comes, open better business will

*from Cleveland'
wide the door —
come in with him."*

THIS LINE FROM A 1904 ADVERTISEMENT IN THE CLEVELAND TRADE BULLETIN exemplifies the optimism manufacturers placed in their products and in their sales force. A group of local manufacturers published The Cleveland Trade Bulletin to inform retailers about the products that they offered and about changes in the industry. Devoted to dry goods, clothing, millinery, knit goods, and boots and shoes, the manufacturers wanted its readers to know that the man from Cleveland selling them cloaks offered a superior product. The journal facilitated connections among the salesmen who traveled the region and country selling their products. The man from Cleveland selling what the workers made was the final step in the manufacturing process. For decades retailers across the country welcomed him warmly.

Top salesmen at Joseph & Feiss, 1920s. (Joseph & Feiss Company, WRHS)

The Work and the Workplace

ONE OF THE STRENGTHS OF THE GARMENT INDUSTRY IN CLEVELAND WAS ITS DIVERSITY. As a regional center, Cleveland garment firms were either cut-and-sew factories or those that made knitwear. Both kinds of firms acquired the raw material, fabric or yarn, from other companies using that raw material to make the clothing they sold to retail outlets. Some companies sold clothing under their own labels, while others worked as contractors, producing for other companies. Maurice Saltzman started in the industry at Lampl Fashions in 1934, in the shipping department. Saltzman explained how the industry worked in an oral history interview:

> *You were either what they call a jobber, which was a sales outfit, or you were a manufacturer selling to a jobber. That's the way distribution worked in those days. Then as time went on distribution changed where they were no longer a jobber. The man who wanted to buy something bought his own yarn, and he went to a manufacturer who was like a contractor, and said, look I want you to make this garment, and I want to make so many dozens and this is the price I can afford to pay for it, now if you can make it I will give you an order. And that is how it worked.[1]*

Adolph. J. Farber. (WRHS)

Herman Friedman. (WRHS)

The manufacturing processes of each type of firm differed significantly. Firms like Joseph & Feiss and Richman Brothers made Cleveland an important center for men's wear, while Printz-Biederman, Bobbie Brooks and Dalton were major names in women's clothing. Some firms, like Ohio Knitting Mills, manufactured both men's and women's clothing, placing the name of another company on the final product. Others, like Campus Sweater and Sportswear, had their own label and also contracted from other manufacturers. Prominent knitting mills included Friedman Blau Farber, Standard Knitting Mills, and Lion Knitting Mills. Friedman Blau Farber incorporated in 1904 with the principals H. Friedman, W. S. Blau, A. J. Farber, Max J. Farber, and I. Whitelaw; Friedman and Blau had been in knit goods since 1883. [2] Each firm needed specialized machinery to make its own goods but often cooperated with outside workers and firms.

The industry presented several challenges to the immigrant entrepreneur. The desire to wear unique garments that were mass-produced required the entrepreneur to specialize and to keep up with technological innovations. Specialization and innovation helped sell the product, the business owner's main goal. The differences between men's and women's clothing challenged manufacturers. Style has always been much more important than fit in women's wear, while fit rather than style has been important in men's wear. In short, women's fashions changed much more quickly than men's styles, with each new

From the scrapbooks of the L. N. Gross Company. (Louis N. Gross, WRHS)

fashion necessitating a change in the manufacturing process. Those changes sometimes meant that new machines had to be installed, which also meant that workers had to be trained. Neither the industry nor the specific manufacturing processes ever stayed the same.

The entrepreneur Louis N. Gross, founder of the L. N. Gross Co., explained in his autobiography the need for flexibility in the industry. Arriving in New York from his home in Ukraine in 1890, Gross was surprised to learn that his brother and brother-in-law performed manual labor in the garment industry.[3] A teacher and private tutor in the Russian Empire, Gross initially sought clerical work in the United States. But his brother-in-law trained him as a cutter and he began his lifelong career in the garment industry. Once he realized the opportunities, Gross turned himself into a businessman, leaving the world of tutoring behind. When he came to Cleveland to work with Root-McBride in 1896, he was dismayed to learn that this jobbing concern was making over fifteen different kinds of garments. Realizing that the firm would never be as profitable as it could be, he left to start his own business. The L. N. Gross Company was the first manufacturing house in Cleveland making only ladies' shirtwaists and dresses.[4]

Standard Knitting Company also learned the benefits of specialization. In an article on the success of the Standard Knitting Company, The Cleveland Trade Bulletin explained the reason for the company's growth, one that must have applied to other manufacturers as well. Established in 1901 by O. F. Schmidt, who had experience in the knitting mills of Europe, the Standard Knitting Company produced both ladies' blouses, jackets and skirts and men's and boys' sweaters. Highlighting the company's remarkable growth, The Cleveland Trade Bulletin wrote, "Following a broad, progressive policy and concentrating their energies upon a class of knit goods for the retail trade, upon which the merchant can clear a good profit and find a ready sale, is the principal reason for their rapid progress."[5] Firms had to specialize in order to maximize their profits. Mass-producing garments of one type was much more profitable than making multiple lines of various kinds of garments.

The garment industry changed rapidly, as technological innovations improved the supply of the products and the nation's population increase propelled demand. Companies specialized, merged and

The Cleveland Trade Bulletin, 1905.

Joseph & Feiss Co. at West 53rd Street between Train Avenue and Walworth Avenue, ca. 1920. (Joseph & Feiss Company, WRHS)

expanded on a regular basis. Older and larger firms bought smaller companies and increased their resources. Moritz Printz, an Austrian Jewish immigrant who had started as a designer of women's cloaks for D. Black & Co. in the 1870s, established Printz-Biederman in 1893, as a partnership with his sons Alexander and Michael and his son-in-law Joseph Biederman. In 1905 the firm, with almost 800 employees, acquired the Sampliner Cloak Company, with less than 200 employees. This made Printz-Biederman the largest cloak manufacturing concern between New York and Chicago. D. Black & Co. spawned another firm as well. David Black's nephew Herman established H. Black & Co. in 1883, makers of women's Wooltex coats and suits, another leader in the field.

Louis N. Gross also saw the need for partnering with others, but was less successful. His first partner died an early death, and the second tried to take over the company on his own.[6] The firm stabilized when Gross' reputation in the business helped him to secure a loan to buy the partner out. The connection between the firms was sometimes physical as well. To ease communication between the workers in various departments, a bridge was built connecting Printz-Biederman and the L. N. Gross building on West 3rd Street.[7]

Competition within the industry presented challenges as well.

Ironing department of L. N. Gross Co., ca. 1930. (Louis N. Gross, WRHS)

And the competition came from all sides, from larger competitors making the same kind of clothing to the smaller workshops. According to a colleague, John Anisfield

complained bitterly of the business and wished himself out of it. I told him that that was only on account of the backward and unfavorable season, but he believes it will never come back to where it was, owing mainly to the Competition of the East Side ki ki cloak makers who are not only ruining the cheap cloak trade but also copy fine goods and kill living profits.[8]

The ki ki cloak makers were those who were employed by manufacturers to spy on the competition, in an effort to determine the fashions other firms would be producing.

Lining department, Joseph & Feiss, 1933. (Joseph & Feiss Company, WRHS)

The most significant challenge, though, was convincing the customer to buy. Many companies followed what seems to be the most standard model. They used traveling salesmen to sell products to retailers across the country. Richman Brothers eventually developed their own stores, selling directly to consumers. Many firms remained contractors, never making and selling clothes under their own label. The contractors agreed to make clothing for

IT'S ALL IN THE FAMILY

By 1920 there were almost a hundred thousand Jews living in Cleveland. Many of them were involved in the garment industry. And many of those involved in the garment industry were related to each other. Family networks and chain migration played an important role in the growth of the industry, helping the industry to stay predominantly Jewish.

The Hays family connection to the garment industry is especially strong throughout Cleveland's history. Kaufman Hays helped to transform the Turner Manufacturing Co., Cleveland's most prominent non-Jewish producer of clothing, into the Cleveland Worsted Mill Co. in the 1890s. By 1920, the Cleveland Worsted Mill Co. had 11 plants throughout the country.

Kaufman's daughter Belle married Martin Marks, also a director of the Cleveland Worsted Mill Co. Bertha Hays, the daughter of Joseph Hays, married Charles Eisenman, founder of the clothing manufacturing firm Kastriner and Eisenman Co. (later Kaynee) and Cleveland's foremost Jewish philanthropist in the early 1900s.

The nephews of Kaufman Hays, who began his career selling remnants of calico, purchased the children's clothing firm Kaynee from their brother-in-law Charles Eisenman. Louis Hays was the President of Kaynee, and a Vice-President of Mt. Sinai Hospital, until his death in 1918. His son Robert Hays took over the leadership of the company until it was sold in 1954. Louis Hays' wife, Jessie Seligman Feiss, was the niece and adopted daughter of Julius Feiss, one of the owners of the men's wear firm Joseph & Feiss. In another connection to the industry, Charles Eisenman was the first cousin of Charles S. Rosenblatt, whose family had established the company that came to be known as Euclid Garment Manufacturing in 1870.

Sometimes different families joined forces, and sometimes these family connections transferred from one city to another. In 1905, Louis Hays of the Kaynee Company and Julius Feiss of Joseph & Feiss founded Federal Knitting Mills Company as a co-partnership. Joseph & Feiss looked to other cities for talent. Felix S. Mayer, a merchandiser from Cincinnati, joined Joseph & Feiss in the 1920s. Richard Adler, President of Joseph & Feiss in the 1960s, came from L. Adler Brothers in Rochester, a company that traces its lineage to well-known family firms in Rochester, Stein-Adler and Stein-Bloch.

Owners of knitting mills had the same family connections. To take just one example, Gary Rand of Ohio Knitting Mills is connected to both Stone Knitting Mills and Frisch Knitting Mills. Harry Stone founded Stone Knitting Mills with Walker Woodworth in 1927. H. E. Frisch married Harry Stone's sister, Pearl Stone. Their son Marc remembers working as a young boy for both his father and his uncle.

Ruth Stone, daughter of Harry Stone, married Leonard Rand. Rand reorganized the Stone firm into Ohio Knitting Mills in 1947. Their son Gary ran Ohio Knitting Mills until it ceased operations in 2004. Similarly, family and personal ties connect other firms as well, including Federal Knitting Mills, Lampl Fashions, Bobbie Brooks, and Dalton.

Charles Eisenman. (WRHS)

Harry Stone, of Stone Knitting Mills.
(Gary Rand, WRHS)

Marc Frisch, in Stone Knitting Mills sweater.
(Marc Frisch, WRHS)

Leonard Rand with his son, Gary.
(Gary Rand)

other firms and pursued contracts with other manufacturing concerns. They provided a range of services, from design to the manufacture of the product. Because these companies never had their own labels, they were never as visible as other manufacturers and never received due acknowledgment for their work. Whatever the route to the customer, the manufacturers faced similar concerns, most importantly, how to stay in business in an industry with a very slim profit margin.

Making the garment itself meant nothing if it could not be sold to a customer. The sales force, predominantly men, linked the factory and the customer. Salesmen had to translate the ideas of the proprietor and designer and the work of the cutters and operators into financial success. To do so, they traveled throughout the country, carrying cases of garments, to make their pitch to retailers in both small towns and large cities. This was as true in the 1960s as it was in the 1860s. The products sold to owners of dry goods and department stores had to respond to the latest trends in fashion and appeal to the retailer. Salesmen concerned themselves with such issues as placement of their products in the stores and, of course, with the quality of the products they were selling. This was difficult work, requiring the building of relationships with retailers to whom they wished to sell again the next season.

At the Clothcraft Store

Model
Y 20

Advertisement for Joseph and Feiss. (Joseph & Feiss Company, WRHS)

L. N. Gross even changed the way his business operated when he came upon an idea he thought would ensure greater sales. Deviating from the norm, he began to rely on a contract system, in which the firm would contract with a single merchant in one location, rather than employing dozens of salesmen to go out in the field. It was the 1910 relocation of The Higbee Co. from its store near Public Square to Euclid Avenue and 13th Street that led to this innovation. Locating the store outside the downtown shopping district of the day, Asa Shiverick, the president of Higbee's, was concerned the public would think the products in the new, relocated store had become too expensive for them. So he arranged to contract directly with L. N. Gross for shirtwaists, eliminating the usual contact with the buyer and the preparation of samples. Gross used this opportunity to create the Wirthmor line, selling the shirtwaist with the slogan one-dollar-worth-more. This sales technique worked for him until sales declined in 1920, when the shirtwaist declined in popularity and the one-piece dress was seen as more fashionable.

The Cleveland Trade Bulletin, 1905.

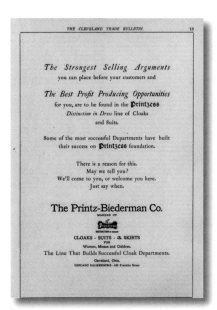

Cleveland's manufacturers united in different associations to support their goal of selling their products. The Cloakmakers' Association is perhaps the best example. Just as the workers themselves organized in local, national and international unions, firms of cloakmakers gathered specialists, proprietors, designers, and salesmen from different firms to reach their goal: "to supply the needs of the retailer so that selling success is sure."[9] Some products were special selling points of the Cleveland cloakmakers because of their success in previous seasons, like the Russian Circular (a fur-lined cloak made on a special machine), Golf Capes (a cloak made of dark material on the outside but colored cloth on the inside) and Satin-Trimmed capes. These different kinds of cloaks simply represented different fashions. They were attempts to appeal to customers in different ways.

The manufacturers' associations also sponsored excursions for merchants to come to Cleveland and view the products available for sale in their retail outlets. The Chamber of Commerce arranged for reduced travel costs so merchants could come to peruse the goods available, including cloaks, suits and skirts, but also dry goods, millinery, china and other products. Similarly, the manufacturers went on trips sponsored by the Chamber of Commerce to meet their customers, retailers throughout the country.

Salesmen were perhaps the employees most attuned to the changes in fashion. The changes often meant new machines or additional training for workers, but they also offered new opportunities to sell. Changes in men's fashion were especially welcome. As reported in The Cleveland Trade Bulletin, manufacturers in April 1905 "prepared varied lines of stiff bosom shirts for men because, while men were comfortably wearing the soft shirt, which looks perfectly proper in summer when the waistcoat is discarded, a man never looks properly dressed when wearing it with a vest."[10] The stiff bosom shirt helped to calm the fear that men's clothing would become a one-season business, which would have flattened demand. Much emphasis was placed on the importance of displaying the shirt in different patterns appropriately: "The trouble is that so many merchants do not place a proper value upon their display. Merchants in the large cities do, and profit accordingly." [11]

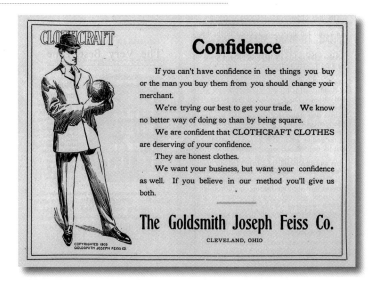

Advertisement for Joseph and Feiss. (Joseph & Feiss Company, WRHS)

LEADERS IN PHILANTHROPY

The success of Kaufman Hays went much further than the garment industry, allowing him an unusually important role in public life. With Myron T. Herrick, Charles F. Brush, and Solon L. Severance, he established Euclid Avenue National Bank in 1886. He ended his career as a Vice President of Union Trust Co. Kaufman Hays also had a role in local politics, most notably stepping in to save the city's credit as acting treasurer in 1888.

The importance of the Hays family and its involvement in philanthropy is difficult to overestimate. Charles Eisenman, husband of Bertha Hays, who was the daughter of Joseph and niece of Kaufman, was the first President of the Federation for Jewish Charities (today's Jewish Federation of Cleveland), established in 1903.

Kaufman's daughter Belle married in 1885 a young businessman from Wisconsin, Martin Marks. His involvement in the Federation for Charity and Philanthropy stemmed from his experience with the Federation for Jewish Charities. His suggestions and experience enabled the success of the Federation for Charity and Philanthropy, success that came about because of the idea to raise money for causes regardless of their connections to Protestant, Catholic, or Jewish organizations. This idea of federation, of joining together to raise and allocate funds, was not unique to Cleveland, but it was Cleveland's organizations, including those mentioned above and Cleveland's Community Chest, that showed how successful federation could be. The Hays siblings and their children moved on from peddling. They and their families achieved a remarkable degree of financial success and integration into the community just a few decades after settling in Cleveland.

Jewish Federation
OF CLEVELAND

Employees of L. N. Gross
Co., undated. (WRHS)

Ultimately, it was the customer in the store who mattered. Retailers passed on their information about what was being most favorably received. For example, elbow sleeves in women's wear were popular in 1905, not least because "the coats made in this style have a distinct character that recommend them to buyers who are in search for goods to give sprightliness to their displays." [12]

Garment makers knew that they could not offer extremes in fashion. In the mass market, they had to provide garments in different styles and fashions to appeal without shocking the sensibility of the customer. They had to care for more than just how they made their product. They also had to think about how that product would be marketed at the point of sale. A sprightly display could make all the difference.

The Workers

EACH WORKER IN THE INDUSTRY PERFORMED A SPECIFIC TASK, which, taken together, added up to a cooperative enterprise that could turn a slim profit. Only a few workers would move on to found garment manufacturing concerns of their own. Many more gave their work in exchange for a foothold in this country that could allow them to find better jobs later and to improve their family's circumstances. Immigrants met the labor need of America's garment manufacturing centers. The wealth those in the industry created for themselves and others helped to transform the city, just as their presence alongside a diverse community of other immigrants presented challenges and opportunities for the growing metropolis.

Louis N. Gross began the closing of his autobiography with the following assessment of the immigrant population:

> *For a young man or woman to leave his native land and travel thousands of miles to a strange and foreign country, whose customs and language he does not know, requires a certain courage, energy and determination. The mentally and physically weak and the sick, lacking these qualities, remained at home. It is the choice individuals from each country who helped to lay the foundation of this prosperous country.*[13]

Gross' assessment of the characteristic of the immigrants may be romantic, but immigrant workers did help the country to prosper economically. These immigrants came primarily from eastern and southern Europe. Some had skills from similar work experiences, whether that meant embroidery at home in their village in Italy or cutting or sewing in a garment manufacturing center such as Lodz, a Polish city under Russian rule. Those from Europe who ended up in the garment industry in the United States, as owners or workers, came from a variety of backgrounds. Some were illiterate, while others were highly educated. What they shared in America was the need to find work quickly. Their contributions to the American economy changed our lives in both dramatic and subtle ways. An example from outside Cleveland is well-known to anyone wearing trousers. Jacob Youphes, a Jewish tailor from Riga, Latvia, is responsible for a dramatic transformation in the modern wardrobe. The blue jeans he invented, made in partnership with Levi Strauss, have become nothing less than a symbol of America.[14] Less dramatically, but with no less consequence, other immigrants simply found work, making clothing. They went on to support their children and families, enabling them to pursue countless versions of the American dream.

Richman Brothers, Detroit, 1930s.
(Robert Harger, WRHS)

In addition to the German and East European Jews who made such a mark on the garment industry, those who came were Poles, Hungarians, Czechs, Slovaks, Slovenes, Croats, Serbs, Italians, Greeks and others. When these immigrants arrived in the late nineteenth century, the frontier town of Cleveland had turned into a bustling city with an increasingly diverse population. By 1890, three-fourths of the city's population was either foreign-born or the children of parents who were foreign-born.[15] Cleveland grew quickly as a result of this immigration, becoming the nation's fifth largest city in 1920, with just less than 800,000 in population.[16]

These immigrants came for all kinds of economic opportunities and worked in all kinds of industries. Many found themselves making clothing because of the low barriers of entry into the industry. Chain migration, reaching back to the old country to bring over friends and relatives, helped the garment industry grow. Mary Barnett Gilson saw this in her role as supervisor of the Employment Department for Joseph & Feiss. She "began to think that all the inhabitants of Bohemia had been tailors, for there was an endless stream of cousins and uncles and aunts of our Bohemian workers who said they had worked as tailors in the old country."[17] While the proprietors of most of the garment industry firms were Jewish, the workforce reflected the new ethnic diversity of the city.

The 1916 survey of the garment industry by the Cleveland Foundation found that for every 100 workers, 47 were machine operators, 23 were hand sewers, 10 were pressers and ironers, 7 were cutters, and 4 were foremen.[18] Men dominated some of these tasks, while women dominated others. Nearly all of the designers and cutters were men. In most cases, machine operators and hand sewers were women. The gender divisions within the industry were not necessarily what one might expect. Many men were machine operators and hand sewers, just as many women handled the work of pressing and examining. Gender divisions varied by city as well, an indication that one cannot make hasty conclusions about the kind of work performed and those employed to perform it. In factories where men performed such tasks as cutting and pressing, it was thought that this occurred because these tasks demanded greater physical strength. The industry gave Jewish women opportunities and exposure to the larger world, and, in this way, contributed to the stability of Jewish families and the development of progressive views among Jewish women.[19]

The garment industry had a presence throughout the city, one that was even more widespread as the companies grew to be more successful. When Joseph & Feiss built a new factory on Swiss Street (later West 53rd Street) in 1905,

The corporate culture of Richman Brothers seems to have extended beyond the employees of the company. When George Richman died, his wife Edith prepared for the funeral to be held in the Temple Memorial Funeral Home, run according to Reform Jewish guidelines. She asked the owners of the funeral home to have an open coffin and a viewing. The owners explained that this was never done in the Jewish tradition, but Edith Richman was adamant. She knew that Richman Brothers employees would want to pay their respects and that they would expect to see George's body. The owners acquiesced. The mother of Edie Hirsch, who tells this story, spent time with Edith Richman at the funeral home.

Oswald Kromer conducts a time study with the seamstress Rose Csaky at Joseph & Feiss, 1920. (Joseph & Feiss Company, WRHS)

the site was selected with the idea of securing a better class of workers than it would be possible to obtain in a manufacturing district. With such a location many persons are attracted who would object to working in shops in the crowded downtown district, and these are mostly of a class that make skillful workers and desirable employees. Then, too, it benefits the worker, as it saves carfare and time.[20]

Likewise, when Richman Brothers opened its new factory on East 55th Street in 1916, its impact on the neighborhood was considerable. The company became an industrial anchor for the nearby Slovenian community.

The Woodland neighborhood, roughly Scovill, Orange and Woodland Avenues between East 22nd and East 55th Streets, provided a home for the Jewish and Italian immigrants who worked in the garment industry.[21] This was the neighborhood that "became synonymous with clothing worker unrest", according to Lois Scharf, a historian who wrote about an important strike among garment industry workers in Cleveland in 1911. But workers and manufacturers became associated with other neighborhoods as well. Surveying the garment industry for the Cleveland Foundation in 1916, Edna Bryner wrote, "Some years ago the contracting shop district of the city known as Newburgh was the great industrial training center for workers in the clothing industry in Cleveland."[22] Newburgh, southeast of the city center, was home to many Poles and Czechs who set up home workshops for many of Cleveland's garment manufacturers. Irish, Welsh and Manx immigrants were among the original settlers of the township of Newburgh, an early rival to Cleveland in the first decades of the 1800s. By the late nineteenth century Polish and Czech workers transformed the ethnic character of the neighborhood

Smoke and grime characterized the inner city of Cleveland in 1910. The influx of immigrants continued to increase. Housing was crowded. Single family homes were divided to accommodate others. More affluent residents began to leave the city for a cleaner environment and larger homes. The city needed social workers.

In 1910 Martin A. Marks of the Cleveland Federation for Charity and Philanthropy, Dr. A. R. Warner of Lakeside Hospital, and Jas. F. Jackson of Associated Charities petitioned Western Reserve University for the establishment of a school to train social workers. That school was founded in 1915 and is today known as the Jack, Joseph and Morton Mandel School of Applied Social Sciences. Its connection to the garment industry? Martin Marks began his tenure as Director of the Cleveland Worsted Mill Co. in 1902. Marks' father-in-law, Kaufman Hays, had helped to turn around the Turner Manufacturing Company in the 1890s, building it into the Cleveland Worsted Mill Co. Marks was also involved in the insurance industry.
Martin Marks, around 1895. (Nancy Jacobs)

Street scene, around 1915.
(Howard Israel, WRHS)

(forming part of today's Slavic Village), and home workshops were a part of the landscape. Though such workshops were on the decline at the time of Bryner's survey, they provided a living for many immigrants.

Ethnicity is central to the story of the garment industry, not because the ethnic groups collided in conflict but because the industry, especially the larger firms such as Joseph & Feiss and Richman Brothers, played a significant role in Americanization. The Joseph & Feiss Clothcraft bulletins illustrate the role of the company in the employee's Americanization. One article, "From Russia to American Freedom", by Jacob Applebaum, described the author's story as a soldier in the Russian imperial army.[23]

Clothcraft vamps, 1923 (caption taken from photograph). (Joseph & Feiss Company, WRHS)

Discouraged by the living conditions he faced as a soldier and unwilling to go to the front, he deserted the army and bribed an agent at the Austrian border, after which he made his way to Antwerp and then to the United States. "When I arrived in this country," Applebaum wrote, "I made up my mind to do any kind of decent work to make a living and become useful. As I had no trade, I got a job with a manufacturer of children's jackets, to whom I paid $10 for learning the trade."[23] Applebaum ended his story with a paean to America, knowing his audience would sympathize with his views.

The factory aided and abetted Americanization. In one short, humorous note, the editors of the bulletin noted "Isidore Spero claims the rare distinction of being the only married Clothcrafter who has never washed dishes or scrubbed the floor for his wife. We always thought that this was an important element in Americanization. How did you miss it, Izzy?"[24] Apparently married Clothcrafters all washed dishes and scrubbed floors at home, having adopted new social roles.

In her role at Joseph & Feiss Gilson observed how workers maintained their ethnic ties and how they gradually adapted to the rapidly changing city they lived in. The workers had their own connections, living in the same neighborhoods and working in the same factories. When an entire line of pressers failed to show up one morning at Joseph & Feiss, Gilson took the company's home-visiting car to visit the district where they lived. She found them playing in a band that was marching in a funeral procession throughout the neighborhood.[25] As Gilson related in her memoir,

> *…the factory demonstrated its functions as a melting pot when time was given for the melting. Evidently melting was welcomed in some quarters. 'My mother was a Poleand she married a Pole," said a girl to me one day. 'Now she says we got enough Poles in the family and I should marry Antonio Augustino if I want to.'*[26]

As the industry grew, so did tensions between labor and management. Strikes occurred in 1904, 1909, 1911, and 1918, and then again in later periods, especially the 1930s. By 1911, the industry had grown significantly; 80 percent of the garment workers in Cleveland were working in factories, not in small home workshops. Working conditions were perhaps somewhat better than in New York, where the Triangle Shirtwaist Factory fire of March of that same year left people with images of women jumping from the building to their deaths. But wages were low and hours were long, and the workers were not organized.

The International Ladies Garment Workers Union (ILGWU) formed in New York City in 1900 and soon after

Beryl Peppercorn treated both laborers and manufacturers fairly. A co-founder of Cleveland's chapter of the Amalgamated Clothing Workers in America in 1914, Peppercorn came to be revered by both workers in the industry and the manufacturers. Peppercorn was twelve years old when his family came to the United States from Austria in 1899. He was just fifteen when the family settled in Cleveland and he went to work for Douglas Tailoring Co. By the mid 1930s, he had succeeded in negotiating contracts with most of the major manufacturers in town. (WRHS)

47

"700 Fussy Tailors" came to be known as a sign of Richman Brothers Quality. To expand his business while insuring quality, Henry Richman, Sr. hired fussy tailors and let them do their work. Richman Brothers produced affordable, high quality suits because they maintained a focus on quality over the decades. Advertisement from *Di yidishe velt*, 1913.

had several affiliates in Cleveland. The ILGWU, founded by workers who spoke Yiddish, saw itself as the industry's melting pot, as an advocate for the many workers in the industry who had come from around the world and found themselves in the needle trades.[27] The ILGWU faced significant difficulties in establishing the unions in the Cleveland area, another indication of the relative strength of the manufacturers in the city. In 1904, local affiliates in Cleveland called a strike against Printz-Biederman without the approval of the ILGWU. At issue was the notion of the closed shop, the demand that the shops be closed to all but union labor.[28] The strike failed and was a real setback for the union cause. The ILGWU continued its attempt to organize workers in Cleveland and in 1910 made the city a focus of a sustained campaign.

Strikes in Cleveland involved spies and outbreaks of violence. Approximately 6,000 workers in 33 firms went on strike in June 1911. Among other demands the workers struck for a 50-hour week with no work on Saturday afternoons or Sundays, no charges for the use of the machines they operated, and no subcontracting. The employers rejected these demands, and the strike dragged on into mid-October. The ethnically diverse character of the workforce made itself visible during the strike. Labor leaders appealed to workers in Yiddish, but many others on strike were Bohemian or Italian. The strike was also marked by violence, some of which was instigated by the employers. The Cloak Manufacturers Association even hired someone to be a spy in the midst of the Picket Committee.[29] Morris Lubin was a non-union cutter who encouraged strikers to take a more militant stance. Lubin was convicted and sentenced for his role in promoting violence after the conclusion of the strike. Meanwhile, employers simply turned to shops in smaller cities to meet the orders placed by their customers. Remarkably, the strikers held out for quite some time; it was only lack of funds to support their cause that made them go back to work in October.

The 1911 strike revealed class divisions as well, especially among women. Any labor unrest in the industry necessarily included women as key participants. Lois Scharf, the author of an important article on the 1911 strike in Cleveland, titled her article on the strike "The Great Uprising in Cleveland: When Sisterhood Failed." As Scharf points out, the wealthy and middle-class women of the Council of Jewish Women did not come to the defense of their working-class sisters. Scharf makes the argument that the Jewish women who were the leaders of the community were also the spouses of the owners and so did not support the significant numbers of Jewish women on strike. Both upper-class and working-class women had strong connections to this important industry.

The 1911 strike highlighted the fact that the industry in Cleveland was always part of a larger world of manufacturing outside of the city. The cloth had to be bought and brought to Cleveland, and then it had to be sold beyond the city's borders as well. National and international organizers worked to consolidate local support for strikes such as the one in 1911. But workers were not the only ones with contacts elsewhere. Manufacturers survived the strike because of their use of workers from outside the city and their use of factories in different towns. During this period of growth in the industry and later in the twentieth century, both manufacturers and workers had contacts outside of the region that often influenced what happened in the city.

From scrapbook of 1937 strike at Federal Knitting Mills. (Richard S. Campen, WRHS)

The strike of 1911 was only the beginning of the union organizer's work in Cleveland. That strike served to alert management of workers' discontent, and that discontent did not disappear. The next significant strike in Cleveland came shortly after America entered World War I. The strike of the summer of 1918 threatened the production of military uniforms and necessitated the involvement of Newton D. Baker, the Secretary of War and former mayor of Cleveland. Most of the larger companies were involved in the war effort and not part of the labor unrest in 1918, which primarily affected smaller shops. The lLGWU had been trying to organize Cleveland's workers since 1911. Its effort proceeded in fits and starts. Just as it gained ground among workers, employers would grant concessions, such as a 48-hour workweek and modest wage increases, and the union lost members.

By 1918, cooperation between the ILGWU and Cleveland's local unions, officially unaffiliated with the ILGWU, had improved. The workers called for a strike in July 1918. They demanded a wage increase from the companies associated with the Cleveland Garment Manufacturers Association. Secretary of War Baker became involved because of the importance of the garment industry to the war effort.

An agreement that included a wage increase and an improved method for settling piecework rates was reached. Baker's truce allowed workers to go back to work in August 1918. However, workers balked when the wage increase was modified. Though they returned to work less than a month after the strike was called, they continued to try to modify the agreement. A final agreement was reached in 1919, but employers would continue to challenge the principle of collective bargaining in the next decades. Significantly, the well-known firm Printz-Biederman insisted, successfully, that they be excluded from this agreement.

Sidney Walzer started in the garment industry in 1918 and eventually worked as a cutter for more than 30 years. He remembered 1918 as the year the union came to Cleveland. According to Walzer, "there was no effective union until they started organizing about 1918....Before the strike in 1918 management did not yet recognize the union – there was no contract signed. But when we went back to work there was a contract. As a result of the strike we got an increase in pay, the union was recognized, and it has existed from that time on."[30] The strike failed to unionize much of the industry in Cleveland, but it began a process of back and forth between management and labor that would result in unionization during the next decades.

Growth and Innovation

WORLD WAR I HAD A SIMILAR EFFECT ON THE INDUSTRY AS DID THE CIVIL WAR. The war effort required garment manufacturers to make changes in production, and these changes led to significant advances in the industry. Men from America's diverse ethnic groups went to battle and donned the same uniforms, challenging the makers of those uniforms to design clothing that actually fit them and that served the purpose of the soldier at war. The military measured its men, and garment manufacturers pressed into serving their country to make uniforms learned more about what fit and what did not. Standards developed, and sizes became more reliable. The demands of war also required manufacturers to innovate. Manufacturers had to design garments that could be worn in different climates, so the weight and quality of the fabric was important. For example, certain kinds of lining repelled lice more than others. Repelling lice helped the soldier to be comfortable. A well-designed and well-produced uniform made a difference in the soldier's ability to fight.

The war led to a significant temporary change for one firm in Cleveland. Richman Brothers opened an expansive new facility on East 55th Street in 1916. Less than a few years after it opened, the factory served a completely different purpose than the one it was built for. Richman Brothers leased the factory to the government for use as a war hospital for a dollar a year. The agreement allowed the government to occupy the building for the duration of the war plus 90 days. While Richman Brothers offered their factory as a hospital to treat wounded soldiers from the Cleveland area, the Mayor's Advisory War Committee sought another, albeit smaller, location for the company for the duration of the war. They found one at the Willys-Overland Company on East 68th Street and Euclid. Workers did not go back on the job on 55th Street until 1919. The war disrupted the operation of the firm but did not keep it from later success.

The next decades saw continued growth for the industry as entrepreneurs continued to develop new product lines and improve their marketing. Samuel Rosenthal, an immigrant from Austria who came to the United States in the early 1890s, founded The Cleveland Overall Company in 1914. Making simple overalls for workers, the company prospered. The pattern of growth and innovation that would characterize the company through the decades was apparent early on. The company acquired the National Railways Uniform Company in 1919. That same year Cleveland Overall introduced the design of a one-piece coverall in 1919 that was more versatile than the bib overall, which required multiple garments be worn underneath. In 1921 Rosenthal came up with an especially innovative idea, renting the garments the company produced to the industries that bought them.[31] Rosenthal had figured out a way to serve his customers. Like other successful entrepreneurs, he offered something new, something his customers wanted and needed. This first attempt to innovate succeeded remarkably well. But by 1921 the price of work wear had decreased markedly. Retailers like Sears were selling overalls as a loss leader, as a way to get people into the shops and then sell them other goods at higher prices. In response, Rosenthal innovated again. The Buckeye Garment Rental Company became the foundation of the company's later success. Not only did The Cleveland Overall Company make the uniforms; they rented the same uniforms to the companies that had bought them previously. They guaranteed the market for their product. In doing so, they helped to create an industry.

From scrapbook of 1937 strike at Federal Knitting Mills. (Richard S. Campen, WRHS)

The L. N. Gross Company faced an even greater struggle. The company's Wirthmor line performed successfully until sales declined drastically in 1920. Gross was then forced to dismiss all of the firm's nearly 1,200 employees. Many on the Board of Directors left at this time as well, not trusting Gross to rebuild the firm and unwilling to incur further losses. Gross did, however, come back. Still in possession of two plants, the firm began making a completely different product, women's cotton wash dresses. The success of these simple dresses enabled L. N. Gross to keep his firm up and running, for decades to come. Gross did not retire until the 1940s, seeing the firm through the Depression.

The knitwear industry saw significant growth in the 1920s and 1930s as well. Newcomers such as Stone Knitting Mills, founded in 1927 by Harry Stone and Walker Woodworth, and H. E. Frisch Knitting Mills, founded in 1929, joined such longstanding firms as Bamberger-Reinthal, Friedman Blau and Farber, and Federal Knitting Mills. Both Stone and Frisch emerged from the bankruptcy of The Rich-Sampliner Knitting Mills Company. Harry E. Frisch took a typical route into the industry. He was a successful salesman for Rich-Sampliner when the firm went bankrupt in 1928. He then took a chance and struck out on his own.

THE LUCK CO.

Richman Brothers' 17-acre tailor shop, on East 55th Street. (Robert Harger, WRHS)

Going into business was not easy. Frisch needed the right equipment in addition to the money and the guts to take a chance. He bought 10 Ketten-Stuhl machines, special machines that made a popcorn pattern stitch. In his reminiscences of this time in the garment industry, Frisch's son Marc explained how the machines enabled his father to make a living:

> *The machines were fed yarn by usually two large beams that were created from individual color yarn cones from a warp wrapping and then rewinding to the beam. The finished knit fabric was steamed, folded and sewn, packed and shipped to several New York companies that cut and sewed and made dresses and blouses.*[32]

Getting into the industry required the capital to acquire the machines that workers could operate.

Harry Stone had worked his way up at the Rich-Sampliner Knitting Mills Company from floor sweeper to head salesman. When Rich-Sampliner closed, Stone and another Rich-Sampliner worker, Walker Woodworth, also decided to go into business on their own.[33] Woodworth had supervised the plant for Rich-Sampliner and so Stone and Woodworth must have thought they would make a good team, one working sales and the other managing the operations. They located their business in the National Screw and Tack Company building, a large complex on Stanton Avenue on the city's East Side. They focused on men's clothing, including pullovers, cardigans and shirts.

Circular Jacquard transfer machine at Frisch Knitting Mills, 1960s. (Marc Frisch, WRHS)

Many of the apparel firms did surprisingly well during the Great Depression, and they were able to keep many people employed during the country's worst economic downturn. David Reinthal, of Bamberger-Reinthal, explained the fate of the company during the Great Depression:

> *From 1921 to 1932, it is my understanding that the company was quite successful and did quite well doing both men's and ladies' sweaters, knit headwear, and so on. With the depression the company did very well.*

*Making very inexpensive ladies'
dresses and men's, ladies', and
children's sweaters. And the fact
that there was an economic
depression in the early thirties,
helped Bamberger-Reinthal rather
than hurt it because they could
make cheap clothing that people
seemed to want.*[34]

**H. E. Frisch Knitting Mills Co. started by making piece goods,
specializing in fabrics made using Ketten-Stuhl machines. They
added other types of machines as their business expanded,
including Raschel and circular transfer machines. The types of
machines they acquired over the years tell the history of the
company. The company also used links machines, TJI machines,
and Bentley transfer and Bentley links machines. These machines
helped the firm produce sweaters for both men and women.**
(Marc Frisch, WRHS)

Frisch Knitting Mills survived
the crisis by innovating. To keep the
factory going, Harry Frisch manufactured a multipack dishcloth, Pearl-
Kleen, named after his wife. Business
was so brisk for Stone Knitting Mills
that the company opened another plant
in Pottsville, Pennsylvania, in 1935.
Richman Brothers, too, was doing well
in the thirties. The company went two
full years, between 1933 and 1935, with
no work stoppages. The story of Arthur Dery, a Hungarian Jewish immigrant, offers another example of
success in the midst of the Depression. Dery started at Federal Knitting Mills as a young man in the 1930s
but then left to work for Excelsior Knitting Mills. When Excelsior fell on hard times, the daring young
man made a bold and successful offer to rescue Excelsior from its financial distress. His move paid off, and
he ended up with half of the company.[35]

While economic depression and labor unrest unsettled the industry during these years, the
garment industry and its influence in the city continued to grow. Making cheap clothing people seemed
to want and could afford was, as many local industry leaders later observed, the key to the success of the
industry in Cleveland. The manufacturer in Cleveland was practical. One industry executive summed up
the outlook for women's suits in 1934:

*After all, if a woman needs a new coat, the first thing that she'll buy is a new coat. She will not substitute a
suit for it. She may want a suit and may buy one later but her first purchase, dictated by good sense and
practical wearing value, will be a coat. A suit is plus business. Suits will be sold to women who already own coats.*[36]

**The *Cleveland Trade
Bulletin*, 1905.**

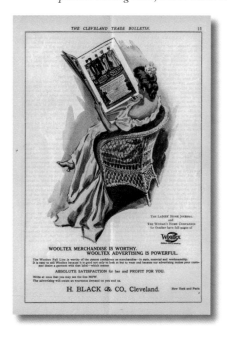

The focus on practicality helped Cleveland's
garment manufacturers to survive, and even prosper, during
the economic crisis.

The success of the garment industry helped to
solidify the position of the Jewish community in Cleveland.
By the first decade of the twentieth century the Jewish
community had become much less fragile than it was when
the immigrants from Germany started their businesses in the
1840s. By the late nineteenth century Simpson Thorman and
Kaufman Hays had already played significant roles in the
governance of the city, as city council member and acting
treasurer, respectively. Recent Jewish immigrants from the
Russian and Austrian empires ended up working in factories
owned by other Jews. Some family-owned firms had already
moved on past the first generation.

In addition, Jewish community organizations formed to address specific needs of the Jewish community. Many of these efforts were the result of the charitable work of German Jews who came to the aid of the Jewish immigrants from Eastern Europe. While Jewish community leaders integrated into the general community, they also formed the synagogues, literary societies, day-care associations, educational groups, community centers and social-service organizations necessary for their community. The arrival of East European Jews helped to transform the community, making the need for separate social services all the more apparent and eventually contributing their time, talent and, ultimately, treasure to important causes.[37]

Four of the nine founders of the Federation of Jewish Charities in 1903 – Charles Eisenman, Julius Feiss, Emil Joseph and Martin A. Marks – had connections to the garment industry. These men became leaders in the community, in both business and philanthropy. The rag trade was responsible for their wealth and for the well-being of many within the Jewish community. While great wealth facilitated the largesse of the philanthropist, weekly salaries insured that recent immigrants could make a living and feed their families. In short, the garment industry made the philanthropy of the Jewish community possible.

Jewish community leaders in Cleveland and throughout the United States were pioneers in the concept of federation, in which donors give to a single fundraising body that then distributes the funds to specific groups. The groups give up their own solicitation efforts to receive the funds. The new Federation of Jewish Charities united the fundraising efforts of eight groups: the Jewish Orphan Asylum (later known as Bellefaire Jewish Children's Bureau), Montefiore Home for the Aged, Denver Hospital for Consumptives, Council Educational Alliance (later the Jewish Community Center), Infant Orphan's Mothers Society, Council of Jewish Women, Mount Sinai Hospital and the Hebrew Relief Association (later Jewish Family Service Association). This more efficient way of raising funds contributed greatly to the success of each of these organizations.

Jewish community leaders participated in other local organizations that also served as federations of commu-

The wealth generated by the garment industry enriched the community in many ways that are easily overlooked. Philip (Fishel) Nashkin was born in Grodno, in the Russian Empire, in 1888. He learned to be a tailor there and came to Cleveland in 1907. In the early 1920s Nashkin founded the Nashkin Cloak Co., on Superior Avenue. He closed the business when he retired in 1958. While he made his mark in cloaks, his passion was the Yiddish theater. He was performing plays, monologues, and comedy routines, in Yiddish, as early as 1912.

Nashkin was devoted to the Yiddish language, and he helped to found the Yiddish Kulture Geselschaft (Yiddish Cultural Society) of Cleveland. The group produced two or three major productions per year throughout the 1920s and 1930s. Nashkin Cloak Company, Prospect and East 4th building. Philip Nashkin is standing at the extreme right, ca. 1925. (Mrs. David Guralnik; WRHS)

The Jewish Orphan Asylum on Woodland and East 51st Street, later known as Bellefaire Jewish Children's Bureau, one of the many institutions supported by the philanthropy of garment manufacturers. (Special Collections, Michael Schwartz Library, Cleveland State University)

nity service organizations. Martin A. Marks was a "prime mover in founding the Federation for Charity and Philanthropy in 1913—first in the nation, but ten years younger than the city's Federation of Jewish Charities."[38] Cleveland's federated fundraising bodies were early examples of cooperation among philanthropists. They helped to channel the generosity of donors in the Cleveland area to social service agencies and became crucial to the support of those in need throughout the region.[39] Success in the garment industry enabled many of the manufacturers to participate significantly in general community causes.

Sewing floor of Richman Brothers, late 1920s.
(Robert Harger, WRHS)

Cutting a pattern, Richman Brothers.
(Robert Harger, WRHS)

"I learned to speak
Isn't that

English.
worth striking for?"

AFTER THE CONCLUSION OF THE KNITTING MILLS STRIKE OF 1937, a forewoman asked a Bulgarian worker what she had gained in 10 weeks on the picket line. Her response: "I learned to speak English. Isn't that worth striking for?" Rose Pesotta, the ILGWU leader who spent the summer of the strike in Cleveland, recounted this incident in her telling of what happened at that time.[1] Many of the companies in Cleveland provided significant benefits for their workers. These included English-language lessons and, sometimes, wages above union scale, yet the workers weren't always satisfied. As the industry grew, workers organized. Employers met their demands, and, in many cases, their businesses continued to grow throughout the mid-twentieth century.

Vest department on sewing floor of Joseph & Feiss, 1932. *(Joseph & Feiss Company, WRHS)*

The Grooming of Model Workers

THE IMAGE OF THE INDUSTRY IN THE CITY STEMS FROM THE RESPONSE OF GARMENT MANUFACTURERS TO THE QUESTION OF HOW BEST TO PROVIDE FOR WORKERS. The answer to this question came sometimes from employers and sometimes from unions. Ultimately, the unions won this argument, but several firms in Cleveland, especially Joseph & Feiss, Printz-Biederman and Richman Brothers, pioneered innovative approaches to labor relations. Ameliorating working conditions and offering significant medical and educational benefits did much to help workers adjust to life in the United States, to improve their socioeconomic standing, and to forestall labor unrest. The unions, however, eventually developed into competitors for the delivery of these benefits.

The demands of the industry necessitated cooperation with other business leaders and, perhaps most importantly, with employees. The sweatshops that seem so characteristic of the garment industry only tell part of the story and, in any case, are not necessarily representative of the workers' experiences in Cleveland. Companies such as Joseph & Feiss, Printz-Biederman and Richman Brothers were known for the favorable conditions they offered employees.

The companies discussed here instituted policies best described as

Teaching English, Joseph & Feiss, 1916. (Joseph & Feiss Company, WRHS)

paternalistic. Indeed, the history of management-labor relations in the industry in Cleveland is an especially interesting one. As the experiences of workers in Joseph & Feiss, Printz-Biederman and Richman Brothers illustrate, garment manufacturers cared for their employees in a number of ways. Not least among the efforts of the manufacturers were the campaigns for Americanization, including the teaching of English and the cultural opportunities provided by many companies. The company became a significant part of workers' lives, an anchor in a city in the midst of roiling change. Because of the paternalistic policies of many of the firms, the organized unions were significantly weaker than one might suppose.

The natural conflict between labor and management reveals the unrelenting pressures faced by manufacturers to make enough money to stay in business and to make a profit. The history of the industry in Cleveland includes at least three ways workers and owners attempted to address their respective interests: collective bargaining, scientific management and industrial democracy. Collective bargaining – the process of negotiation between workers and employers in an effort to resolve disputes over wages or working conditions – is really only one model of management-labor relations. Local leaders in the industry also tried other models, including new twentieth century business trends such as the scientific management of Frederick Taylor and the industrial democracy of John Leitch. The paternalism of these models ultimately gave way to collective bargaining in Cleveland. In the end, the employers' idea of what workers needed was not enough to meet the demands of workers. Scientific management succeeded for Joseph &

Feiss for many years, just as industrial democracy worked for Printz-Biederman. Paternalism did leave its mark on the industry in this town, significantly limiting the success of unions until the mid-1930s and leaving behind an important chapter in the history of labor-management relations. But workers ultimately turned to collective bargaining to resolve their differences with their employers.

The paternalism of employers reached deep into workers' lives. Companies offered programs that essentially supported, enriched and monitored both the physical and mental well-being of their employees. It is true that the employers did so at least partly because they wanted to improve production and keep out union activity, but it is also true that they were remarkably successful in providing for employees' needs. The presence of the unions in the garment industry was never as strong in Cleveland as one might suppose, precisely because the programs offered by the employees were so effective, and thus so popular. Before the growth of unions and government regulation on employers, many companies in Cleveland provided their employees, many recent immigrants, with access to such benefits as medical care and recreational, educational and cultural opportunities. Employees took advantage of the benefits and participated in the programs enthusiastically. The dinners, picnics, holiday parties, concerts and theater performances became an important part of their lives. Such offerings provided opportunities for employees to bond with each other and with the corporation of which they were an important part.

A vice president in charge of organization and manufacturing at Joseph and Feiss, Richard A. Feiss aimed to improve his company's bottom line and the lives of his employees. By 1912 Feiss, a graduate of Harvard Law School, had become well-known as a proponent of scientific management, the idea that workflow could be regulated and managed more effectively. Time and motion studies of repetitive tasks could help managers figure out the most efficient processes and protect employees. Feiss wrote about such issues in *Forbes* and *Harvard Business Review* and took steps to implement his views at his family's firm.[2] Two women helped him. The first was Emma Brittin, who spent two years putting the company's welfare programs in place.[3] Then the remarkable Mary Barnett Gilson came to Cleveland in 1912 at Feiss' invitation. Gilson, from a comfortable family in Pittsburgh and educated at

---

Lizzie likes her job! That was the conclusion of John Commons, a progressive labor historian who wrote the following description of the work at Joseph & Feiss in 1920:

In a great well-lighted structure, nimble fingers are guiding hundreds of garments under the needles of power-driven sewing machines. A quick turn, a break of the thread, a toss to the left while picking up another garment at the right, and each girl bends forward again as the cloth speeds thru the machine.

In rapid succession girl after girl arises from her place, carries the bundle of garments she has sewed over to a nearby table, walks to the control board in the center of her division, has her work recorded and receives another batch of garments to work on.

The measurements of the scientific managers at Joseph & Feiss impressed Commons. So too did the play hour, when married and unmarried women played tug of war or other games. Joseph & Feiss in 1920 was, according to Commons, a model of management-labor relations. (Joseph & Feiss Company, WRHS)

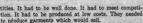

Ninth article in the Independent's Industrial Series on the big plants that are finding a successful answer to the problems of labor unrest

Lizzie Likes Her Job

By Professor John R. Commons of the University of Wisconsin

In collaboration with A. P. Haake, O. F. Carpenter, Malcom Sharp, Jennie McMullin Turner, Ethel B. Dietrich, Jean Davis, John A. Commons

IN a great, well-lighted structure, nimble fingers are guiding hundreds of garments under the needles of power-driven sewing machines. A quick turn, a break of the thread, a toss to the left while picking up another garment at the right, and each girl bends forward again as the cloth speeds thru the machine.

In rapid succession girl after girl arises from her place, carries the bundle of garments she has sewed over to a nearby table, walks to the control board in the center of her division, has her work recorded and receives another batch of garments to work on.

They work hard, these girls, and they work steadily. The garments literally flow thru the shop in an unbroken stream. One gains the impression that some omniscient being has arranged all the machinery, so delicately adjusting its parts that everything operates in perfect coördination and balance with every other part.

For this group of six hundred workers, most of whom are women and girls, the turnover for employees, after the probation period of five days, has averaged about 5 per cent per month over a period of six years, the range being between 33.5 per cent and 67.02 per cent per year. The absentees average about 2 per cent per day, and many of the women are married and have their own homes. More than two-thirds of the entire group have been employed here more than a year, while over 15 per cent have served ten years or longer. The workers are healthy, their appearance is neat and business-like. There are no strikes, production has steadily mounted, and wages have increased more than the increase in labor costs. The factory runs with the full force the year around.

Joseph & Feiss understood the art of designing clothes and measuring cloth to fit the pattern so as to utilize most of the cloth. Likewise, they designed the kind of an operative force they needed for their business and proceeded to measure the human beings to fit the design. They needed work done in large quan-

titles. It had to be well done. It had to meet competition. It had to be produced at low costs. They needed to produce garments which would sell.

If the factory could be kept running without lay-offs one great source of loss could be overcome; it would mean less waste of overhead expense and smaller turnover of labor. But it was difficult to accomplish this so long as dealers bought goods in season and so long as changes of style made over-production an ever-present menace.

They proceeded to educate their salesmen and their trade. First their materials and later their styles were standardized to meet a certain extensive conservative demand, principally for the more serviceable and every-day man's clothing. These models change very little, standardization lowers the cost, and it becomes feasible to manufacture the garments before they are actually sold rather than wait for orders. They develop their market to absorb a year-round production and make possible the economies of continuous production.

Fitting the operative force to the production design meant a measurement of human motives. How can you induce Lizzie Meyers to fit herself in with a scheme of scientific production, appear for work on time every morning and work steadily for the entire day? How can you get her to keep the quality up and the stream of production unimpeded, at the same time keeping her happy and loyal, willing to remain in your employ even when another employer tries to attract her to his company?

Lizzie is a bundle of motives and if you appeal to the proper motives with just the requisite appeal you win; if not you lose.

But you cannot measure motives with a yard stick as you can cloth. Incentives, motives, human willingness to do things, all grow out of mental states. It was discovered, however, that you can measure motives in terms of dollars and cents. For money makes possible the gratification of most desires and provides a measure of the attitude of human beings to each other. [Continued on page 202

Mr. Feiss has made his factory "the greatest experimental laboratory of industrial psychology"

Next Month—To Their Mutual Advantage

Miss Mary Gilson has a keystone position as head of the service department of Joseph & Feiss

Exercise class, Joseph & Feiss, 1915. (Joseph & Feiss Company, WRHS)

Washroom at Joseph & Feiss. (Joseph & Feiss, WRHS)

Learning to sew. Mary Barnett Gilson oversees Suzanne Fahndrich. (Joseph & Feiss Company, WRHS)

Wellesley, worked in Pittsburgh's libraries before she took a job training young "shop girls." Gilson had seen the circumstances in which library patrons and shop girls lived. She saw the grime and filth from Pittsburgh's industry, and she became interested in how training could help employees better both their professional and personal circumstances. Arriving in Cleveland in 1912, she took on the position of superintendent of the Employment Department and helped Feiss to enact Frederick Taylor's "mental revolution," the revolution needed to make scientific management succeed. Over the next 12 years, she launched policies and programs that dramatically altered the lives of employees and became well-known nationally for her work. Close contact with employees also gave Gilson the opportunity to observe the lives of Cleveland's immigrants. She made home visits, met their parents and grandparents, and knew their boyfriends and girlfriends. Her experiences at

Joseph & Feiss launched her career in industrial relations. She eventually left the factory for academia, but she never forgot what she learned in Cleveland. When appointed a fellow of the Guggenheim Memorial Foundation in 1939, she wrote a memoir of her career, *What's Past is Prologue*, in which she detailed her experiences and adventures at Joseph & Feiss.

Scientific management is the idea that the performance of a worker's task can be made more efficient if that task is studied carefully and the quickest, most efficient way to complete that task determined. Proponents of this idea carried out very precise time studies to determine the best way for an employee to complete a specific task. Such study of specific tasks led to much greater precision from workers, which in turn allowed for greater productivity and increased profits. The idea was to figure out what workers could actually do and how they could improve their work while maintaining their physical and mental health as an employee. Under Richard A. Feiss, Joseph & Feiss was eager to teach employees what they thought their employees should know. The firm implemented various types of vocational education. This included English, an obvious way for immigrants to improve their circumstances and their productivity. But it also included behavior that was deemed civil and proper by the leaders of the firm. Such concerns led to the development of the Employment and Service Department at Joseph & Feiss in 1913. Supervised by Gilson, the department was responsible for the well-being of employees and for many of the examples we still cite today as proof of the manufacturers' concern for workers.

Gilson was as interested in the cleanliness of an employee's fingernails as she was in the straightness of their seams. As a report of the Service Department stated,

> *The shower baths in the Clothcraft Shops are not merely ornamental…The service department constantly strives to impress upon the workers the fact that a truly efficient person will prefer a clean, healthy body and plain, businesslike clothes to untidiness, powder, jewelry, 'rats', and other evidences of false ideals."* [4]

Seamstress at her workplace, Richman Brothers, 1930s. (Robert Harger, WRHS)

Good grooming was not just about a clean body and clean fingernails; it was about ideals of businesslike behavior and efficiency and health. A moral judgment accompanied the soap. In a similarly judgmental tone, the author of the report stated that Joseph & Feiss did not have to prohibit the use of chewing gum, because "the majority of the employees have accepted the fact that it is an unhealthy and disgusting habit."[5]

Nutrition class, Joseph & Feiss. (Joseph & Feiss, WRHS)

Perhaps not surprisingly, Gilson did not approve of women wearing make-up, a habit that was becoming increasingly common. She related in her memoir that some of the employees agreed with her: "Gosh, Miss Gilson, did you see Sylvia Proznik today? She looks like a Polish pine tree dressed up for Christmas." While some employees thought make-up in the workplace was inappropriate, others wanted to wear it. Gilson's example illustrates the intrusiveness of the company's policies, an intrusiveness that at least some of the employees accepted. The attitude toward make-up changed over the years. Gilson later came to regret her insistence on "simple dress" and "healthy natural skins", seeing such insistence as too much interference in employees' personal habits.

The employee bulletin for Joseph & Feiss, known as *Clothcraft* from the company's brand name, offered readers lighthearted general interest articles and information about the company and other employees. The bulletin also told

A CLOSE-KNIT GROUP

Workers were not the only ones to organize. Manufacturers organized, too. The National Knitted Outerwear Association, Cleveland District, was an association of knitting mills in Cleveland, Ohio, originally affiliated with the national group headquartered in New York City. In the 1930s, the Cleveland District withdrew from the National Association and ceased to exist, and local knitting mills joined the national organization as individual members. The Cleveland group had re-affiliated with the national organization by 1960, but they continued their meetings and close collaboration. The primary members of the association included Bamberger Reinthal, Lion Knitting Mills, Stone Knitting Mills (Ohio Knitting Mills), H. E. Frisch Knitting Mills, Excelsior Knitting Mills (Dalton), Standard Knitting Mills and North American Knitting Mills.

This was a close-knit group. By the 1950s the Dery, Frisch, Haber, Hibshman, Reinthal and other families had been in business for decades. The professional association gave them the chance to exchange information, for example, when members visited mills in England or hosted visitors in the industry from the Netherlands.

The nature of the industry necessitated contacts among suppliers and manufacturers and

between manufacturers. The families associated with these companies came to know each other well and developed both business and personal ties. Like the workers, they, too, organized into local and national associations. The National Knitted Outerwear Association is perhaps the best example of how leaders in the industry cooperated and collaborated to improve their products, and their sales.[32] The group formed to allow the manufacturers to share resources and to learn from each other about best practices in the field. Members participated in dinners, lectures and golf outings as well.

One of the group's joint endeavors was a testing laboratory, created and originally housed at Lion Knitting Mills. All of the Cleveland mills were invited to use this facility until they set up their own laboratories. The lab tested the quality of fibers and helped manufacturers determine their options for making new products and their existing products better. Synthetic fibers transformed the clothing we wore, how it was made and how we wore it. Because of their ability to adapt, companies that had been established for decades continued to grow, while others were just embarking upon decades of success.

employees how to behave. Readers learned about how to shower and even how to fold a paper towel when washing their hands.[6] The method outlined made it possible to dry the hands with just one paper towel, not two or three. Two photographs of rows of chairs and tables in another issue taught workers about order. One photograph shows the chairs all at different angles from the table. The other shows the chairs neatly pushed in. The caption asked readers which was more neat and tidy. The answer was implicit in the photograph. John Commons, one of the most important labor economists of the Progressive Era, wrote that Joseph & Feiss was "the greatest experimental laboratory of industrial psychology that we have found in America."[7]

The firm offered employees other kinds of lessons, too. The Cleveland Public Library established a branch at the factory, and the report of the Service Department stated that workers used the small library of 400 books often enough to insure that new titles were always available. The library included volumes on business and management, but the Service Department did not insist upon non-fiction reading. Workers could make their own choices.[8] The firm also offered cultural opportunities, too, encouraging their employees to participate in celebrations, theatrical performances, folk dances, ballroom dancing and other events. Workers organized some of these events themselves. The firm provided the space and allowed workers to organize events such as folk dances after regular working hours. The Service Department described such events in its report:

Local talent is encouraged in music and recitations and the different nationalities are always eager to dance their dances, the psenicka of the Bohemians and the czardas of the Hungarians being the most popular. Folk dances such as the Swedish clap dance and the Danish dance of greeting are enjoyed by all and very frequently the evening's fun is increased by a little pantomime, an exhibition of 'fortune telling' or some other performance carried out by members of the section.[9]

1308 Russell Road, in the St. Clair-Superior neighborhood, around 1915. (Howard Israel, WRHS)

Managers, superintendents, and forepersons participated in such events as well, just as they did in the exercises and ball games held at the noon hour. Many employees often recalled these events affectionately years later.

Americanization was an important priority for Joseph & Feiss. Employees had "to learn to talk and think 'United States'. "[10] Joseph & Feiss clearly viewed Americanization as an important endeavor and even as another benefit that employment at Joseph & Feiss could offer workers. In addition to the cooperation with the Cleveland Public Library, the firm also worked with the Cleveland Board of Education. The Board provided five English teachers to teach late afternoon classes to Joseph & Feiss employees, so they would not have to go home and then go out again to a night course. Joseph & Feiss procured professional teachers for their employees and accommodated their schedules. The goal of these courses was not simply the speaking of the language. Language was not simply language. It was also Americanization. The cooperation with the city also suggests just how important this Americanization was for both the immigrants and society more generally. City institutions cooperated with a private company to meet the pressing need of a significant segment of the city's burgeoning population.

Perhaps one of the reasons that the paternalism at Joseph & Feiss was so extensive was because most of their employees were "girl needle-workers" and not "husky and oftentimes obstreperous men workers".[11] Young women,

As a student at Harvard, Richard Feiss counted the number of steps from his dorm room to his classroom, testing various routes until he found the one that was most efficient. A Forbes profile of Feiss revealed that his was the ideal temperament to take up Frederick Taylor's ideas of scientific management. After reading Taylor's work, Feiss wrote to Taylor to describe what he and his family were trying to do at Joseph & Feiss. Taylor responded. He had heard of the company and so was interested in what was happening in Cleveland. The two began a productive friendship, and Feiss eventually became President of the Taylor Society. (Joseph & Feiss Comapny, WRHS)

often in their late teens, needed much of the help provided, and the firm saw a real benefit to its bottom line from training their workers appropriately. Significantly, they also sponsored a visiting day during the week for family and friends of employees. This taught management more about the worker's family circumstances, and this helped both the firm and the employee. For example, management learned that many of the young girls were not even opening their pay envelopes. They simply turned over their pay to their families. When they realized this, they encouraged the girls to save a portion of any wage increase in the firm's Penny Bank for themselves.[12] Management must have seen this as an especially significant advantage of employment at the firm, since "thrift is the very foundation of success and happiness."[13]

The paternalism of Joseph & Feiss extended to a concern for the living conditions in employees' private homes. A report of the Service Department described the housing of employees on the West Side and Broadway Bohemian district.[14] Many employees lived in small one- or two-story style frame houses, some with enough yard space to care for chickens, ducks and geese, especially important for the Bohemians. Family members preferred to sleep together in back bedrooms or kitchen areas, leaving a large parlor room free "for bric-a-brac and family portraits." Over all, the houses were "remarkably clean and well-kept," but, as one might expect, crowding was sometimes an issue. Some homes had small houses in the rear where boarders or family members could stay. Extended family members usually lived in the other living quarters of the two-story houses. As one woman said, "I am going to move out of this neighborhood for the foreigners are buying up all the houses around here and making regular tenements of them." Neighborhoods that were otherwise well-kept faced challenges posed by the city's remarkable rise in population (which apparently included chickens, ducks and other fowl as well as people).

Henry and Nathan Richman with employees, 1929. (Robert Harger, WRHS)

American workers in the twenty-first century may find it difficult to imagine the presence of the company in workers' lives during this time. Companies such as Joseph & Feiss offered such far-ranging benefits and services that many employees were bound to the company in significant ways. Employees depended on the company for a paycheck, access to inexpensive meals, medical care, English lessons, and educational, recreational, and cultural opportunities of all kinds. In short, the company intruded on the lives of its employees to a degree we would not recognize or countenance today.

Gilson's Employment and Service Department at Joseph & Feiss conducted home visits. She visited the homes of employees when they were absent or if there was a significant issue to address. These issues included relatives who drank, spouses who had become difficult to deal with, and unexpected pregnancies. Gilson always had the welfare of the employee and the company in mind, but it is difficult to disentangle her concern for the worker from her concern for the company. Gilson believed strongly that developing informal relationships with the employees would help them overcome difficulties and, as a result, to be better workers.

Together, Feiss and Gilson transformed the relationship between owners and employees and set an example for Cleveland's other firms. Joseph & Feiss attracted international attention and became known for their successful experiment in industrial relations. However, when they faced an economic slump in the early 1920s, Feiss and Gilson had to reckon with the reality that not all of their company's leadership supported their views. Gilson grew uncomfortable with the discrepancy between the pay of executives and the pay of workers, especially at a time when some of the company's activities were cut back and some employees were laid off. She resigned in 1924, understanding that the company would not be able to withstand the economic pressure without further cuts, and resenting that her work was increasingly described as simply "frills and furbelows." [15] Gilson went on to become an economist at the University of Chicago.

Richard A. Feiss was in the uncomfortable position of holding views in opposition to those of his father, Julius Feiss, and his brother, Paul Feiss. Opposed to scientific management, Julius and Paul Feiss gained the support of the company's other executives and Richard A. Feiss resigned in 1925. The company's experiment had ended.

The executives at Printz-Biederman experimented as well. They followed the ideal of industrial democracy, in which workers participated in the management of the workplace. Based on the ideas of the labor theorist John Leitch, industrial democracy allowed workers a voice in the management of the workplace.

Industrial democracy as implemented at Printz-Biederman mimicked, to an extent, the structure of the government of the United States. The Senate, comprised of the company's leadership, was the higher chamber. The House of Representatives, because it consisted of representatives of the people, or the workers, was, however, no less important. The bylaws of the House of Representatives outlined the function of the House of Representatives:

> *...to study and recommend action to the Senate as shall be concerned with the production of good coats and suits at the lowest possible cost; the payment of highest profits, salaries and wages consistent with competitive ability and betterment of social and physical conditions among the people of the Printz-Biederman Company.*

This unique attempt to address the interests of workers helped to make Printz-Biederman one of the city's most successful companies.

> The workers of Printz-Biederman sat out the strike of 1918. Alexander Printz was justly proud of this, because the workers' position reflected the positive working conditions that were a result of his implementation of industrial democracy. That form of governance evolved since its adoption in 1914. Four years later the Senate had been abolished. In its place was a Planning Board made up of department heads. Printz-Biederman successfully lobbied to be excluded from the agreement made between the strikers and the factories in 1919 because of their successful management practices.

Sign in store window on West 29th Street, across from Federal Knitting Mills, during 1937 strike. (Richard S. Campen, WRHS)

The House of Representatives addressed one of the most pressing problems of the industry, the problem of the slack season, "a time of the year where we are not able to keep the entire force steadily at their work." These periods arose because customers desired various kinds of clothing at different times of the year. Employment in the industry was often seasonal, one of the most important of workers' complaints. At an April 1915 meeting, the House decided that they would recommend that new employees who had not shown themselves to be capable of the company's standards be let go first, while the hours for everyone else would be reduced. Thus, all workers shared the cut in pay through the slower season equally.

Employee representatives listened to talks from the company's leadership at the meetings of the House of Representatives, but they also addressed very specific issues related to their work. The House intervened when cutters complained that dividends were not being distributed fairly or when Jewish workers requested compensation for time off on Jewish holidays (a request that was ultimately denied). The owners of Printz-Biederman were Jewish, but they did not offer time off for Jewish holidays. Printz-Biederman employees were invested in both small details and more significant issues related to the running of the shop. The company's House of Representatives addressed such issues but had limited power to effect real change. In spite of its efforts to involve workers in company decisions, Printz-Biederman was a frequent target of union organizers. Paternalism did not always satisfy workers' needs.

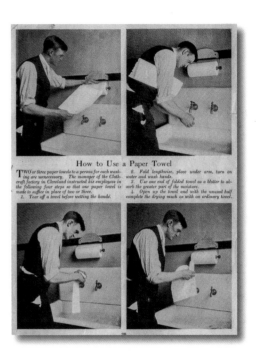

How to Use a Paper Towel, from the Joseph & Feiss Company Records, undated. (Joseph & Feiss, WRHS)

Given the kinds of opportunity and oversight provided by firms like Joseph & Feiss and Printz-Biederman, it is perhaps appropriate to wonder about the proper roles of such companies in the lives of employees. The Clothcraft bulletins show that the company was or could be involved in most aspects of an employee's life – education, day care, recreation, vacation, and social and cultural activities. The experiment in industrial psychology being conducted in these factories occurred in the midst, or perhaps because, of the period of greatest immigration to this country. Both managers and employees knew that the diversity of the workforce had to be managed. Simply offering employment served neither the owners nor the workforce. Employees needed to learn English, to learn about American customs and institutions, both for themselves and simply in order to perform their jobs more effectively.

The factories adopting these policies attracted attention. Those inside the industry had a vested interest in determining the success of these policies, but the general public found the policies intriguing as well. In May 1917 The Temple-Tifereth Israel Women's Association planned a trip to the factory of the Kaynee Co. on Aetna Road. The bulletin for this excursion noted that the streetcar journey would take about 45 minutes and that attendees would be able to see the schoolroom, playgrounds, library, hospital, dental laboratory, kitchen, lunchrooms and laundry of this model factory.[16] These facilities were evidence of the paternalism of the industry, a topic of interest as early as 1917.

Not all firms were so paternalistic. L. N. Gross Co., for example, took the position that "most of our executives felt our obligation was to compensate our people at the highest possible rate, and then let each person take care of her

After the effects of the Depression and subsequent labor unrest, Cleveland's apparel firms formed the Cleveland Fashion Institute in 1938 to promote the industry. A local newspaper explained the reason for the new organization:

Fighting against something intangible, the leaders of the $50,000,000 industry saw factories and wholesale houses begin to fold up, their owners retire or move to other cities, partly because labor conditions were unhealthy, partly because buyers began to take their business to New York and Chicago exclusively. Under the direction of local businessman and public relations executive Jacob Wattenmaker, the Cleveland Fashion Institute launched Cleveland Market Week. The week of fashion shows gave local manufacturers a chance to market their wares to buyers from Cleveland and throughout the region. The Cleveland Fashion Institute, a forerunner of Fashion Week Cleveland, folded in 1940. (James Wattenmaker, WRHS)

Notice for meeting of knitting mill workers during 1937 strike, Federal Knitting Mills. (Richard S. Campen, WRHS)

or himself." [17] The company did, however, sponsor picnics, evening dinners, and Christmas parties for its employees, much as did Joseph & Feiss, Printz-Biederman and Richman Brothers. Employees at L. N. Gross had access to lunches at a nominal cost and a small circulating library and showers. The company also set up moving-picture equipment during the lunch hour for short films. More significantly, L. N. Gross advocated the establishment of a national unemployment insurance fund. The Gross executives' position that they should simply offer the highest rate of pay is noteworthy. Not all manufacturers viewed their employees in the same way as the leaders of Joseph & Feiss and Printz-Biederman.

Scientific management and industrial democracy ultimately failed because they could not offer the workers a voice that was truly independent of the interests of management; they simply could not stand up to the pressure of organized labor. These approaches to management-labor relations addressed the needs of the workers, but they regarded the interests of management and labor as one and the same. Collective bargaining allows workers a voice to fight for what they need. The tension between management, labor and representatives of organized labor troubled the industry for many years and continued after World War I.

The Right to Bargain

L IKE JOSEPH & FEISS AND PRINTZ-BIEDERMAN, MANY MANUFACTURERS HAD VERY EXPLICITLY TAKEN STEPS TO PROVIDE THE KINDS OF BENEFITS WORKERS WANTED. But simply providing these benefits or setting up an internal organization could not ensure the manufacturer would hear the concerns of the workers. The New Deal reforms of the 1930s, especially the National Labor Relations Act of 1935 (the Wagner Act), empowered workers to organize. During the strike of 1911, a writer for the *Cleveland Press* editorialized, "Back of the strike lies the question of the right of the garment workers to form a union for the improvements of their conditions. It seems a late day for the denial of this right, but apparently there are still a few employers who have not learned it." [18] The same was true in the 1930s.

In the eyes of one worker, the union helped to ensure good working conditions. Harley Goldstein asked his grandfather Sidney Walzer to tell him about his years of work in the garment industry in a 1983 oral history interview.[19] In Walzer's telling, the union came in just when Walzer started

The strikes in Cleveland sometimes led to altercations among strikers, strikebreakers, and police officers. There were instances of vandalism, arrests, and beatings. Strikes often brought violence that threatened both workers and owners. Strikes were a last resort for workers, the tangible evidence that the relationship between workers and management had frayed and broken down. A description of the picket lines at L. N. Gross on February 16th, 1935, tells of the danger owners sometimes faced: *About 2:15 p.m., a Mr. Gross was observed walking south on West Third Street, and as he neared the plant one of the members of the Truck Drivers' Union, who was pretty well intoxicated, shouted 'here comes Gross, let's get him'. This man, as Mr. Gross will probably recall, deliberately tried to bump into him and in the meantime police officers stationed nearby made no effort to intercede.*

Printz-Biederman employees could dress just as well as the company's customers. From "Rules Governing Employees" at Printz-Biederman:

You have the right to purchase garments at regular wholesale price for your wife, mother, sister, or daughters if living under the same roof....Purchases of raw materials, such as lining, cloth, etc., can be made in a similar manner...

Robert Ebert remembers that his mother and grandmother could still purchase coats and suits at a discount after the death of his grandfather who worked in maintenance at Printz-Biederman.

(Judah Rubenstein, WRHS)

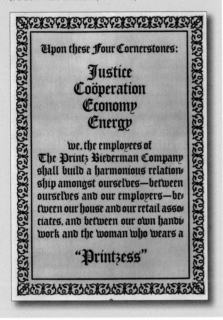

Upon these Four Cornerstones:

Justice
Coöperation
Economy
Energy

we, the employees of The Printz Biederman Company shall build a harmonious relationship amongst ourselves—between ourselves and our employers—between our house and our retail associates, and between our own handiwork and the woman who wears a

"Printzess"

work at M. T. Silver, a firm that made women's coats and suits, in 1918. His first job in the industry was timing the cutters as they performed their various tasks. Walzer worked at several companies throughout his decades-long career as a cutter, including Keller and Kohn, Printz-Biederman, and, for a brief time, Joseph & Feiss. Long hours for the same or lesser pay bothered Walzer more than the physical condition of the factories where he worked. Throughout his oral history, he repeatedly stated that the conditions in the places where he worked were modern and sanitary, attributing this at least in part to the role of the union after 1918. Walzer told his grandson,

The environment in all of the shops was modern. They had fans. All of them had fans. You know, you were uncomfortable at times. Cutters had to work standing up. You couldn't do it any other way. The only time that you could sit down was when you took a break. You could take breaks — in the morning a few minutes and a few minutes in the afternoon — but otherwise it was a standing job.[20]

The demands of the industry, however, did keep Walzer from completing his education. Sidney Walzer explains how long hours kept workers from secondary and advanced studies. Walzer told his grandson,

The regular workweek was 48 hours long and we worked a half-day on Saturday. Later on the union started becoming more active, and they cut the hours down. But, earlier, you had to work overtime sometimes to 7 p.m. or so. It was too hard to go to school and work these hours at the same time, so I had to quit school.[21]

Walzer entered the industry at a time when it had already matured. Employers had already established benefits and programs for their employees. Organized labor had already begun to win concessions on wages and hours. As the unions established a stronger presence in Cleveland, they began to offer workers some of the same kinds of educational and recreational opportunities and healthcare and insurance benefits. Paternalistic practices could not stave off worker discontent inevitably.

The national and international unions that formed in the first decades of the twentieth century came to Cleveland and fought, successfully, for the right to bargain collectively.

INJUNCTION NOTICE

Only Three Pickets allowed here by Order of the Court

All persons will take notice that on February 1, 1935, His Honor, J. P. Dempsey, Judge of the Court of Common Pleas of Cuyahoga County, in case No. 420,935, pending in said Court, entitled The L. N. Gross Company, plaintiff, v. Abraham W. Katovsky and others, defendants, issued an order enjoining the following acts:

"*congregating on the streets or sidewalks of West 3rd Street in front of plaintiff's property or in the immediate vicinity thereof, or on West 4th Street, for the purpose of or with the effect of preventing plaintiff's employees or others from entering said factory; provided, however, that the defendant Abraham W. Katovsky, or in his absence from the city the defendant Louis Friend, for and on behalf of all of the defendants, may station three (3) pickets, consisting of two (2) women and one (1) man, or three (3) women, at or near the West 3rd Street entrance of plaintiff's factory, and three (3) pickets, consisting of two (2) women and one (1) man, or three (3) women, on West 4th Street at or near the entrance to plaintiff's private driveway, whose activities shall be and they are hereby limited to peaceful persuasion and observation.*"

VIOLATORS OF THIS ORDER ARE PUNISHABLE BY THE COURT AS FOR CONTEMPT.

The L. N. Gross Company

Injunction notice in L. N. Gross strike, 1935. (Louis N. Gross, WRHS)

Henry Richman, Jr., Nathan Richman, Charles Richman, 1920s. (Robert Harger, WRHS)

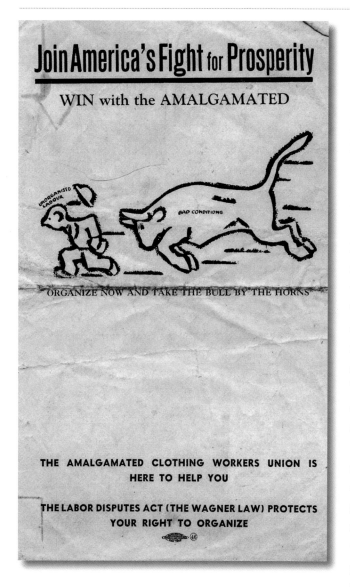

Join America's Fight for Prosperity

WIN with the AMALGAMATED

ORGANIZE NOW AND TAKE THE BULL BY THE HORNS

THE AMALGAMATED CLOTHING WORKERS UNION IS
HERE TO HELP YOU

THE LABOR DISPUTES ACT (THE WAGNER LAW) PROTECTS
YOUR RIGHT TO ORGANIZE

The Amalgamated
Clothing Workers Union is
here to help you.
Organizing material from
the 1920s. (Mrs. Beryl
Peppercorn, WRHS)

Disputes flared up most dramatically in 1933 and 1934. About 1,500 workers in 10 dress manufacturing companies went on strike at the end of July 1933. The strike affected some of the biggest local names in the business, including Bloomfield, Kux-Bleiweiss, Glick Sportswear, Famous Dress Company, and S. Korach Company. Throughout the early weeks of August the strikes concentrated on Bloomfield and S. Korach, because these companies refused to participate in an agreement with the union. Owners resented workers' efforts to influence work at other plants. At issue was the Korach facility in Ashtabula, which struck in sympathy with workers in Cleveland. The opposing parties reached an agreement in mid-August. The agreement increased wages.

According to the Korach family, the battle with the unions took its toll on management. Sigmund Korach was found hanging in the basement of his factory at 2400 Superior in December 1934. Police attributed the suicide to prolonged ill health, but, privately, the family blamed their father's conflict with the union, even suggesting that Korach knew his family would receive a death benefit from the insurance company even in the case of suicide. While the causes of an individual's suicide are certainly complex, it is true that the company ceased operations after the death of its main principal. The precise reasons for the firm's closure are difficult to determine in such trying circumstances. Relatives including Sigmund's son Arthur and the Kux family continued their involvement in the industry in other ways. Arthur Korach worked with Joseph & Feiss and Richman Brothers, before moving to Baltimore to continue his career with L. Greif & Bro., Inc.

The union came to Joseph & Feiss in 1934. The company had been in the forefront of the move to provide benefits to workers, but, as in other non-unionized companies, the workers did not have an independent voice. And the social welfare programs the company sponsored had been cut significantly in the 1920s. In March 1934, two union groups voted to strike Joseph & Feiss.

At issue was the dismissal of a presser who had been let go for alleged union activity, a wage increase, and a demand for recognition of the union. The strike lasted only four days. Sidney Hillman, the head of the ACWA, came to Cleveland to address the Joseph & Feiss workers at the Bohemian Sokol Hall on Clark Avenue and to confer with company officials. The two sides reached an agreement quickly, calling for the National Labor Relations Board to

Both management and workers had to pay close attention to costs. The Welfare Committee at Printz-Biederman responded to increased costs in the company's dining room by raising the prices. Meat went from 5 to 7 cents and potatoes from 4 to 5 cents. These increases were meant to make the dining room a sustainable operation. Portions and quality were to remain the same.

The workers of Printz-Biederman sat out the strike of 1918. Alexander Printz was justly proud of this, because the workers' position reflected the positive working conditions that were a result of his implementation of industrial democracy. That form of governance evolved since its adoption in 1914. Four years later the Senate had been abolished. In its place was a Planning Board made up of department heads. Printz-Biederman successfully lobbied to be excluded from the agreement made between the strikers and the factories in 1919 because of their successful management practices. (Judah Rubinstein, WRHS)

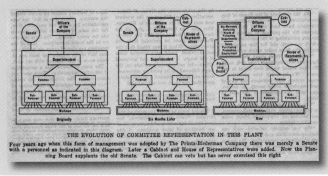

THE EVOLUTION OF COMMITTEE REPRESENTATION IN THIS PLANT

Four years ago when this form of management was adopted by The Printz-Biederman Company there was merely a Senate with a personnel as indicated in this diagram. Later a Cabinet and House of Representatives were added. Now the Planning Board supplants the old Senate. The Cabinet can veto but has never exercised this right

direct an election asking workers to choose who should represent them, the union or a Joseph & Feiss employee plan. If the union were to win, the discharged presser would be reinstated and the ACWA would enter into a contract with Joseph & Feiss. Hillman presented Joseph & Feiss officials with 1,425 union cards, tied in bundles of a hundred with a rose attached to each bundle. He proudly proclaimed, "We have enlisted 1,425 men and women to aid the President in carrying on the New Deal." [22] Unusually, the company requested the vote be held in the company assembly room of Joseph & Feiss, and the workers agreed. The union won. Joseph & Feiss reinstated the discharged worker, workers received a ten percent wage increase, and the union was in.

In contrast, the strike at the Kaynee Co. later the same year was longer and more contentious. Kaynee, too, provided for its workers in some of the same ways Joseph & Feiss had. The amenities Kaynee provided—the classroom, playgrounds, library, hospital, dental laboratory, kitchen, lunchrooms, and laundry—did not ensure positive relations between employer and employee. In 1934 the ACWA brought two cases of discrimination before the National Labor Relations Board, charging that workers had been unfairly targeted because of union-related activities. Workers struck, however, before the National Labor Relations Board could make any kind of ruling. A week after workers went on strike on November 5, 1934, Kaynee closed its three Cleveland plants, located not far from each other in the neighborhood known today as Slavic Village.

Beryl Peppercorn, head of the local chapter of the ACWA, also urged the closing of the Kaynee plant in Bucyrus, Ohio. Owners claimed they closed the plants because of the violence and terrorism that accompanied the strike.[23] In fact, bricks had been thrown through the windows of homes owned by workers who had not gone out on strike.[24] Whether legal or not, the strike had been the workers' way of expressing their impatience. Kaynee and the National Labor Relations Board had to address their concerns much more quickly. The revered labor leader Beryl Peppercorn recognized workers' need for a quick resolution as well.

No settlement was reached, though, until January 1935, when, after negotiations facilitated by the NLRB, the right of the workers to their own union and to collective bargaining was granted. There had been no wage dispute and no demand for a closed shop, but workers were now free to choose to be represented by a union. ACWA's Sidney Hillman was in town again. Once more sounding triumphant, he declared,

The Kaynee cafeteria, 1946. (Michael Louis Hays, WRHS)

THE KAYNEE CAFETERIA

Workers at KAYNEE have no need to go outside for well-cooked appetizing meals. KAYNEE'S modern, completely equipped cafeteria is another reason why KAYNEE is a good place to work.

KAYNEE EMPLOYEES

...are efficient because they can be happy at their work. They have steady, year-round employment at good pay in pleasant surroundings. Manufacturing conditions at KAYNEE prove that high quality and low price can successfully be combined with thoughtful consideration for the well-being of employees.

I am confident that soon every Kaynee worker will be a member of the union…the government demands that industry give security to labor. We are not out of our troubles, but we are seeing a new light. The American people and especially labor are awakening to what can be done.[25]

Moritz Printz and Jos. Biederman, from Printz-Biederman brochure. (Judah Rubinstein, WRHS)

Several of the buildings housing garment manufacturers included other concerns as well. This involvement sometimes exposed the companies and workers to significant danger. Shortly before the end of the era of Prohibition, Max E. Felsman was convicted and sentenced for his part in a "murderous plot" to burn down the factory building at 7500 Stanton Ave., home of Stone Knitting Company and Frisch Knitting Mills. The arson stemmed from Felsman's bootlegging.

While the union came into Joseph & Feiss relatively easily, the conflict between labor and Printz-Biederman was much more confrontational. The ILGWU had been trying to get into Printz-Biederman for decades. But the company's institution of the principles of industrial democracy had served it well and workers were satisfied enough with working conditions that the union did not seem to be an attractive option. Looking back on his days as a labor leader in the industry, Sidney Walzer recognized that some manufacturers offered workers conditions that were indeed satisfactory. Walzer recalled of Printz-Biederman,

There was one shop that it took a long time to get into the union. But, finally, they did get into the union. The workers there were doing pretty good without the union. They did have good conditions. They had a play area there, it was a big place. They didn't get paid too much more, but they worked more overtime than the union shops. Finally, they did get into the union….[26]

Abraham Katovsky, local labor leader in the 1930s, continued to press Aleksander Printz to offer his workers union wage scales. Printz and Katovsky negotiated throughout the summer of 1934. By 1935 Printz had begun to realize that the introduction of the union was inevitable, in spite of his company's solid record of fair and generous treatment of its workers. Because of the tensions surrounding the negotiations, Katovsky asked for an agreement rather than a vote on joining the union. David Dubinsky, ILGWU President, negotiated an agreement with Aleksander Printz that established a local union separate from the Cleveland ILGWU union but affiliated with the international association.[27] The Dubinsky-Printz Agreement signaled that the relationship between labor and management had changed. Without more source material from workers, it is difficult to know just how workers felt about conditions in specific firms at different times. Unions offered enough benefits to prove attractive to employees, who, with the support of organized labor, could express their own needs to the employers.

The next significant strike was even more contentious. The strike of workers in four Cleveland knitting mills in 1937 was a clash between employers and employees and between rival groups of workers.

The picket line at L. N. Gross Company, unidentified newspaper clipping. (Louis N. Gross, WRHS)

SUMMER, decided those on the picket line at the L. N. Gross Co., 1220 W. 3d Street, yesterday, as snow swirled around their ears, would be better than this. In fact, who picket this weather anyway?

A conflict among the International Ladies' Garment Workers' Union, the American Federation of Labor, and the emerging Committee of Industrial Organizations (later the Congress of Industrial Organizations, the CIO) accompanied the Cleveland strike. The strike involved some of the most important local names in the industry, Bamberger-Reinthal, Federal Knitting Mills, Friedman Blau Farber, and Stone Knitting Mills. ILGWU President David Dubinsky and the well-known labor leader and ILGWU Vice President Rose Pesotta gave the strike much attention. At

1220 West 3rd Street. This strike scene at L. N. Gross occurred in January 1935. (Jewish Community Federation, WRHS)

issue was the right of the workers to be represented by organizations of their own choosing. The owners were opposed to organization, and the workers could not agree on which organization(s) should represent them.

The strikes occurred during the summer of 1937, a year that also saw strikes in the steel and automotive industries. Pesotta, a seamstress and labor leader born in Derazhnaya, Russia, came to Cleveland for the duration of the strike and its resolution, from June to October. Photographs of workers on the picket line and of "loyal" workers going in to work made the pages of the newspaper all summer, especially when violence among the workers occurred. Local labor leader Abraham Katovsky missed most of the strike, as he was recovering from an attack by thugs involved in labor unrest in February 1937.

Pesotta herself was on the picket line. She was struck twice, once with a razor above her left eye and then punched in the face. In one of the most dramatic episodes of the strike, AFL workers broke through CIO picket lines at Stone Knitting Mills at 7500 Stanton Ave. on June 30, 1937. [28]

The strike of the knitting mills in 1937 involved a group of workers affiliated with the American Federation of Labor and another affiliated with the newly formed CIO. Many workers affiliated with the AFL went to work during the 1937 strike, and they were identified as scabs. The violence that accompanied the 1937 actions was both among workers and between police and picketers. Temperatures ran high, and tactics were not always fair. In the run up to the strike, men who had introduced themselves as AFL organizers urged workers "to join a 'real' union affiliated with the AFL and not a CIO Communist union like the International Ladies' Garment Workers' Union. That's nothing but a Jew-union dominated by Moscow."[29] The CIO significantly increased its membership throughout the 1930s, partly due to such actions as those in Cleveland in 1937. They faced real opposition, not just from the owners, but from rival unions as well.

Though there was violence between opposing factions of workers, those on strike took care of each other, and the ILGWU took care of its own. The union faced real organizational challenges. Workers needed money and food. Picketers and organizers had to travel from knitting mill to knitting mill, since they were not located in the same neighborhood. Much of the action took place at Federal Knitting Mills, located at West 28th Street and Detroit Avenue, not far from the West Side Market and a local Hungarian parish, St. Emeric Church. As Pesotta writes,

The strike commissary was set up in the Hungarian Social Hall, several blocks from the Federal mill. In a well-equipped kitchen, squads of women strikers prepared food, which was delivered in cars to the four picket lines. Thought of those tasty dishes makes me hungry even now—hot soups, with piquant flavor, Hungarian goulash, home-made sausage, produced dexterously with curious gadgets and broiled to a turn, big loaves of health bread. Soft drinks and coffee were added. On that fare I gained ten pounds that summer.[30]

Both national organizers like pesotta and local leaders like peppercorn made sure that those on strike were taken care of. They managed the gap between the workers' sacrifice for the larger cause of the union and the immediate need for bread. Unions could offer workers the same educational, cultural and recreational opportunities as manufacturers. The conflict between labor and management was at least in part simply a working out of the issue of how Americans would gain access to important benefits like insurance and medical care.

The strike continued until August, when the still relatively new NLRB ruled that elections must be scheduled so workers could choose the organization of their choice to represent them. The ruling was a victory for the workers, whose right to organize independently was recognized. As Pesotta knew, though, it was a hollow triumph, as Federal Knitting Mills closed rather than comply with the order and other companies refused to re-employ the workers who had been on strike. Still, the strikes were another step in establishing the principle that company workers' councils should be illegal. Both the workers and the new governmental regulations of the 1930s recognized that paternalism could not always satisfy workers' demands.

Richman Brothers would remain the significant exception among garment manufacturing companies in Cleveland. The company was never unionized. Over the years, it was the lack of a union that made Richman Brothers stand out within the industry even more than its unique way of doing business. The Richman brothers viewed their employees as family and the "Richman Family" received the benefits of their benevolent paternalism. Richman Brothers instituted paid vacations for its employees in 1919, one of the first companies to do so. In 1920, members of "The Richman Family," that is, employees, became stockholders in the company.

Family became the dominant theme in the company's self-image. In

L. N. Gross workers return to work after 1935 strike, from *The Cleveland Press*, March 8th, 1935. (Louis N. Gross, WRHS)

addition to vacation pay, the company offered the same range of recreational and cultural opportunities as firms like Joseph & Feiss and Printz-Biederman, including participation in and performances by the Richman Family Orchestra, formed in 1922. The company sponsored holiday parties and an annual picnic. Festivities at the picnic included a beauty pageant for many years. Such programs and events helped to bond the employees to the company, but company policies surely helped as well. In 1931, the brothers in charge of the firm gave up their salaries. They then formed the Richman Brothers Foundation, to provide assistance to both employees and to local charitable and social service organizations. The foundation continues to operate today.

The Richman Family image was much more than a marketing ploy. Speaking to the workers at the event celebrating the twenty-first anniversary of the construction of the building on East 55th Street, Cleveland's Bishop Joseph Schrembs praised the Richman plant as

> *the outstanding plant in the country. It not only preaches social justice, but practices it. From all sides, today, we hear nothing else but strikes, sit-downs, and I know not what else. There never has been a strike in The Richman Family! There are efforts being made all over the country to establish trade unions and labor unions. They have their place in society as long as conditions are such as they are today in many of our industries. But they have NO PLACE in The Richman Family...just because you ARE a family.[31]*

Richman Brothers had called on Bishop Schrembs to address its employees because many of them were Roman Catholic. Schrembs spoke directly of the differences in identity of the employers and employees. He noted that the brothers themselves "made no distinction of creed, or race, of tongue" and called on the Richman family to do the same: "How could we love Yosef, Miriam, and Jesus and hate a Jew? It can't be done."

Employess and families at Richman Brothers event, 1950s. (Robert Harger, WRHS)

"As it is, we go in

and out of business every six months."

RICHARD ADLER, THE CHIEF EXECUTIVE OF JOSEPH & FEISS in the 1960s, expressed a truism of the industry in a 1969 interview in *Men's Wear.*[1] What was true for Louis Gross in 1920 was true in 1969. The fortunes of the garment industry ebbed and flowed. Cleveland's entrepreneurs rode a wave of success in the postwar period, but they could not stabilize an industry that by definition is unstable.

Florian Fashions, 1980s. (Marc Frisch, WRHS)

World War II

SOME WORK WAS BEING DONE IN HOMES AS LATE AS 1940. Marc Frisch, whose uncle owned Stone Knitting Mills, recalled, "In 1940, I would deliver knit body fronts to the homes of Italian women in Little Italy who would hand embroider them and I would exchange their finished work with new parts on a next visit."[2] This peaceful existence could not last. Marc's brother Jerry entered the army in 1940, and Marc was drafted in 1943 when he was studying business at Miami University. Marc was not able to complete his education until he returned home from the service.

The war changed the operations of the companies that made clothing, too. The nation needed garment manufacturers during World War II, just as they did during the Civil War and World War I. For example, knit linings helped extend the life of tires, so knitting mills in Cleveland made tire boots for the military during the war. Cleveland-based companies also made uniforms, parts of uniforms, sweaters, caps, helmet liners, nets, and puttees, wrap-around leggings that could be worn by soldiers in the place of leather. Lampl Fashions manufactured parachute parts for the military. Such wartime initiatives required cooperation with the government and significant changes in production. Firms were subject to changing government regulations that limited what they could produce and then sell.

The entrepreneurs of Cleveland's garment industry were happy to offer help to the country that had offered them such opportunity. A few manufacturers were awarded the Army/Navy "E" award for Excellent production records and support of the armed forces. One of those, Joseph & Feiss, produced hundreds of thousands of uniforms for naval officers during the war. The company produced raincoat-overcoats, chief petty officers' uniforms, Navy tropical uniforms and officers' gabardine coats. Production was so brisk they opened a new plant in Utica, New York, in the middle of the war. The raincoat-overcoats were made of 16-ounce serge that was fashioned to be water-repellant. The coat included a wool lining to make it truly all-weather. The tropical uniform was made with a blend of worsted and mohair, called Mohara, to maintain its coolness and shape. The outbreak of the war in 1941 coincided with the company's centennial anniversary, and the firm was justly proud of its more than century-long service to the military, including aid provided during the Civil War, the Spanish-American War, and World War I. Many of the firm's workers also served their country by going overseas to fight. Joseph & Feiss included 152 men and women on its honor roll, three of whom died in service.

One of the best chronicles of the lives of garment industry workers during the war comes from The Majestic Specialties Company. Emery and Dave Klineman, brothers and founders of the company, distributed a newsletter to all of the company's employees serving in the military during the war. Each issue of The Majestic Messenger included a brief update of what was going on at the factory. The editor usually just mentioned employees who were sick or on vacation or who had been on leave and visited Cleveland. Risqué humor and anecdotes about workplace gatherings or parties outside of work kept soldiers reading. The purpose of *The Majestic Messenger*, though, was to distribute the correspondence of the employees.

Jerry and Marc Frisch meet in Paris during World War II.
(Marc Frisch, WRHS)

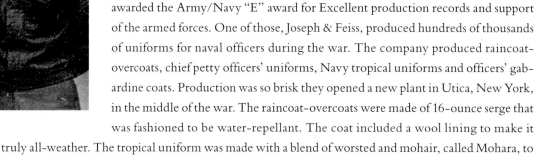

From The Joseph & Feiss Co....in War and in Peace:
One of the most outstanding garments developed under the Naval Officers' Uniform Plan was the Raincoat-Overcoat. The Navy required an all-purpose outer garment which could be worn in any climate. The Joseph & Feiss Raincoat-Overcoat was the answer. The Regulation raincoat, made of the best 16 ounce serge obtainable, was "Cravanette" Processed, so that it was water repellent. The Joseph & Feiss Company produced an all wool lining with sleeves, that could be buttoned into the raincoat, so that with the addition of the lining it had the warmth of an overcoat. Joseph & Feiss quality is known and respected by the hundreds of thousands of Navy officers and chief petty officers who wore the Raincoat-Overcoat.

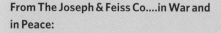

(Joseph & Feiss Company, WRHS)

The first issue appeared on September 25, 1942. The editors were Dave Klineman, Emery E. Klineman, Joe Rossio, Joe Nagy and Bob Klineman. They explained their idea of distributing a weekly newsletter with copies of correspondence sent to them. The first issue was sent shortly after the High Holidays, and the editors noted "everyone seems to have 'dovined' [prayed] well over the holidays, they all seem to have that satisfied look. Some of the bosses lost some of their big bellies fasting on Yom Kippur. This doesn't mean Joe Rossio."[3] The pattern of the news shared by the editors was apparent in the first issue – good-natured joking, comments about the good-looking "girls" in the office, advice to see a movie, notes about employees who had visited or started school or gotten married, etc. The letters were often directly addressed to the Klineman brothers themselves or simply to "Dear Gang" or "Fella voikas [workers]!"

The "off-color yarns (this is the only type of yarn we have left)" proved very popular. *The Majestic Messenger* started out small in 1942, with just about 10 people who were part of the network. At its peak this more or less weekly newsletter was sent out to 135 service members, including Majestic employees (sometimes referred to as Majesticites or Majesticians), former employees, and friends or customers who simply wanted to hear from the young men and women of Majestic and share their own news. Over the years the team behind the newsletter added special features, such as song titles humorously altered or "minute bios" of the correspondents, most of which noted that the employee was a graduate of Cleveland's Glenville High School. The company updates reveal glimpses of how the company's fortunes changed during the war as well, sometimes mentioning that production increased or materials were difficult to obtain.

Taken together, the employee correspondence and updates from the company tell the story of the employees' relationship to the company and their activities during the war. In the first letters the new soldiers write breezily of their time training and waiting for deployment. The company always urged its employees to write, since the success of this venture depended on employees' willingness to participate.

CLEVELAND'S LOFTS

Today it's possible to live where yarn was turned into sweaters. Several of the former factories have become focal points for the urban living so encouraged by Cleveland's city leaders.

Printzess Square, at 425 Lakeside Avenue West, was once the home of Printz-Biederman. Today the building is home to one- and two-bedroom apartments owned by Jacobs Investments. The luxury apartments offer excellent views of the lake and were an important part of the development in the Warehouse District in the early 2000s. Its neighbor, L. N. Gross at 1220 West 3rd Street now houses a bail bonds office and a fast food restaurant.

The Federal Knitting Mills Building on Detroit Avenue and 28th Street, once the site of the most significant labor unrest in the history of the city's garment industry, is residential, like Printzess Square. Residents in the one- and two-bedroom apartments are part of the twenty-first century development of Ohio City. They are within walking distance of the West Side Market and well situated between downtown and the burgeoning Detroit-Shoreway neighborhood.

The buildings along Superior Avenue remain, testament to the physical imprint of the garment industry and home to an array of small businesses and artists. 1900 Superior Avenue, now known as the Tower Press Building, was built for H. Black and Company. The architecturally distinct building included features meant to make the building more attractive for workers. The water tower, decorated with stucco panels, distinguishes the building and marks the start of the area that was once a center of the garment industry. The building became home to the Evangelical Church from the late 1920s to the 1940s. After a series of tenants and companies, the building was vacant until the mid 1980s and its renovation into live/work units for artists and others.

The Artcraft Building, at 25th and Superior, home to such companies as Lampl Fashions and the Famous Dress Company has hosted artists since as early as 1987, when a group of Cleveland Institute of Art graduate students opened a co-operative studio there. (Tomasz Markiewka, WRHS)

Federal Knitting Mills

Artcraft Building

Printzess Square

Tower Press Building, 2013. (Cindy Bruml, WRHS)

Some wrote more than others, but all expressed their appreciation for the chance to learn about what their friends and colleagues were doing and where they were.

As the war progressed, the employees' dispatches mentioned the toll of the war more explicitly. The now experienced soldiers told of their interactions with the local populations and of their time in battle. Rather than bearing the names of places that served as training camps, such as Tampa and Hollywood, the letters came from "somewhere in Italy" or "somewhere in the Marianas." In August 1945 the editors announced, with a note of regret, that they would no longer continue the newsletter. With the ending of hostilities, Majestic employees had returned home and so there was no longer a need for the weekly missive. The company relocated to New Jersey in the early 1950s. The newsletter reveals the concern of the owners for their employees and the close-knit nature of the community surrounding the company. Majestic even made contributions for their employees to the Jewish Welfare Appeal while they were overseas fighting.

The owners and workers of the garment firms were still only a generation or two removed from their European homes. The war sometimes brought them into closer contact with their relatives, who sometimes ended up in the industry. Such was the case in the Lampl family. Joseph Lampl started Lampl Knitwear in the 1920s when he left Federal Knitting Mills.[4] He and his brothers were knitwear jobbers. A true family firm, the company employed three of the family's four brothers and the husbands of their four sisters. The company developed to have several divisions, including Lampl Sportswear, a cut and sew firm, and they became known for knitted dresses and suits, but they also made dresses, suits, and slacks. In the spring of 1938, Carl G. Lampl was contacted by Karl Lampl in Vienna, an operator in the embossing department of Addressograph-Multigraph Ltd. Addressograph-Multigraph was an Anglo-American company with offices in London and Cleveland. Karl Lampl was dismissed from his job with the company in Vienna after the annexation of Austria by Germany in March 1938. He then took steps to get himself and his wife, Leopoldine, out of Austria. He inquired about jobs in England, and he made contact with Cleveland's Carl Lampl. How exactly the two first made contact is unknown, but Carl agreed to help Karl and Leopoldine, "because of the similarity of our names, and the fact that there is a relationship that obviously dates back to beyond that which either one of us can trace."[5]

"Treasure Tones". . . your fabulous new fashion-trove! Jewel-like colors coordinated to mix, match and mate. A wealth of costumes from few . . . for campus, career, casual wear. Sweaters of fine-gauge 100% Australian zephyr wool or crimp-set nylon . . . glorious solid shades and blending heather hues. Skirts dyed-to-match in handsome wool and rayon checks and plaids or wrinkle-resistant rayon sheen gabardine. Sweaters: 34 to 40, about $5 to $9. Skirts: 10 to 18, about $7 to $11.

For name of store nearest you write: Lampl Fashions, Inc., Cleveland 14, Ohio • N. Y. Showroom: 1410 Broadway

treasure tones FASHIONED BY *Lampl*.

(Louise Lampl Butz)

Karl Lampl was sent to Dachau in 1938 and then released with the help of the Quakers. He was eventually able to obtain a visa to England and made it there before the outbreak of war. With help from the Lampl family in Cleveland, Leopoldine Lampl eventually managed to get a visa, too, but only after the war had started. By February 1940 the European Lampls were in Cleveland. By 1945 Karl Lampl was a foreman for the Lampl Sportswear Manufacturing Co. He supervised the pressing, finishing and packing departments. After the war, many survivors and refugees found employment in garment factories, just as earlier immigrants had. Karl Lampl was certainly not the only European refugee to receive help from families in the United States.

When the war was over, young men and women – like Marc and Jerry Frisch and the Majestic employees, but also like young Karl Lampl from Austria – could resume their plans for the future and garment manufacturers could get back to their more usual activities. The postwar economic boom, especially the baby boom, meant that business would be better than ever.

Postwar Growth

B Y 1951, MORE THAN 90 PERCENT OF AMERICANS WERE BUYING THEIR CLOTHES OFF THE RACK. After the austerity of the war, Americans were ready for color and for more casual clothes,[6] and the factories of Cleveland gave them what they wanted. Today, when the factories have closed and, in the case of many, been torn down, the scale of the garment industry in the city is difficult to imagine. But the factories of manufacturers and suppliers anchored neighborhoods on both the East Side and West Side. They were located throughout the city, meaning most neighborhoods included homes of workers who could afford those homes because of their work as cutters, sewers or finishers. Machines in these factories ran up to 16 hours a day. Making sweaters or dresses required massive amounts of raw material. Ohio Knitting Mills alone stored more than a million pounds of yarn when at peak production.

Cleveland's manufacturers distributed the sweaters, dresses and blouses they made all throughout

Career clothes from
Work Wear.
(Lois Wainwright, WRHS)

the nation. Improvements in transportation allowed for easier distribution. Traveling salesmen had already gone far and wide throughout the South and West in the late nineteenth century. They sold their products to small stores in some of the nation's smallest towns. But, increasingly, Americans shopped in larger department stores and then in shopping malls. Clothing made in Cleveland was bought in Sears, Montgomery Ward, J. C. Penney and Spiegel not to mention Cleveland's own Halle's, Higbee's and May Company. According to local entrepreneur Steven Tatar, "It was Midwestern manufacturers – not the high-end designers in New York, Paris or Milan – who determined what the majority of Americans wore."[7] Another local company, Jo-Ann Fabrics, also grew significantly during this period. Founded in 1943 as the Cleveland Fabric Shop by Hilda and Berthold Reich and Sigmund and Mathilda Rohrbach, Jewish immigrants from Germany, the retailer of fabrics went on to become one of the country's largest fabric and crafts stores. Alan Rosskamm, the son of Betty Reich and Martin Rosskamm, ran the company in later years.

Americans learned to be much more casual after the war. The change to casual wear offered significant opportunities to the garment manufacturing companies in Cleveland. The companies faced technical challenges in adapting to this new kind of clothing. The development of sportswear for both men and women allowed some companies to develop special niches. The fashion revolution demanded new sewing machines and knitting techniques. Some products changed almost beyond recognition. Sam Janis, a union leader in the 1960s and 1970s, looked back on his years in the industry and explained at least one reason for the switch to sportswear,

> At one time Cleveland was the second largest coat producing area in the country…Today there isn't a coat factory in Cleveland…When women started to drive cars, they didn't need long coats. All they needed was a short coat, the result was that they would wear a short coat. They didn't want a fancy coat. It used to be that a woman would have a spring coat, and a fall coat, and a fur coat. Now she drives a car and she puts on a little jacket or a short coat up to the bottom of the back, and then she goes out and she is in that car. She finds it very comfortable and convenient…So she didn't need it, she didn't need the product.[8]

Women started driving, fashions changed, and the garment industry responded with innovative products.

Several well-known names in the Cleveland garment industry grew exponentially in the postwar period. The Cleveland Overall Company changed its name to Work Wear when it went public in 1961 and became, arguably, the city's most successful manufacturer of clothing and a pioneer in the industrial laundry field. The city's knitting mills prospered throughout the 1980s. Founded in 1901, Bamberger-Reinthal was nonetheless still a pioneer in the 1950s, when David Reinthal worked with Dupont to create and market a sweater made out of a new fiber, orlon. Frisch Knitting Mills developed new products to respond to customers' desire for more colorful, comfortable, and casual clothing. Ohio Knitting Mills passed from the Stone family to the Rand family and continued to flourish. Dalton, run by Arthur Dery with roots in Excelsior Knitting Mills, became a well-known manufacturer of cashmere sweaters. Bobbie Brooks, the new kid on the block, capitalized on the youth market by specializing in matching sweater sets for juniors. The company created a market for their products and literally changed how department stores presented their products for sale. In addition, Joseph & Feiss, Richman Brothers and Printz-Biederman remained in operation and continued to operate profitably for a few more decades. Both established companies and newer names grew tremendously from the

1950s to 1970s, but they all experienced significant difficulties that eventually led to their sale or closure in later decades.

Under the leadership of Samuel Rosenthal, the Cleveland Overall Company became a pioneer in a related industry. The strategy of renting the uniforms the company produced succeeded phenomenally. This insured a continuing relationship between the customer and the manufacturer that propelled growth through the 1930s. In 1940 the Cleveland Overall Company entered the industrial laundry business. The firm made, rented, and laundered work wear of all kinds. Like other companies, the Cleveland Overall Company also produced uniforms for the military during World War II.

Rosenthal succeeded in providing what we might think of as the most humble garments to have been produced, overalls and uniforms for average workers. But there was nothing average about the quality of the product and the service the manufacturer provided. When Samuel's son Leighton took over the business after his father's death in 1957, he proved to be as much of an innovator as his father. The company then became known as Work Wear. According to Leighton Rosenthal, the war was a stagnant period for the firm. As the nation became more prosperous after the war, unions negotiated better benefits, sometimes including uniforms. Business picked up considerably. Leighton Rosenthal

Advertisement for James Kenrob, a Dalton line. (Arthur, Ken, Jim, and Bob Dery, WRHS)

L. N. Gross made uniforms for employees of amusement parks, including Cedar Point and the now much lamented Geauga Lake. Such work was not such a departure from their lines in women's sportswear. The uniform had to catch the eye and be cool enough for summer but warm enough for the cooler days of early fall. Style and fabric were always of utmost concern, especially for uniforms which would be worn all day and worn out easily.

attributed the increase in business to returning servicemen "who got used to wearing uniforms and expected them".[9] The company's industrial laundry business expanded internationally and exponentially. By innovating and developing the rental and industrial laundry businesses, the company offered industries of all kinds a valuable service, one many companies were willing to pay for handsomely.

Uniforms looked neat and clean on workers, and many business leaders saw uniforms as a way to improve worker morale. Work Wear's overalls became career apparel. The uniform was not meant solely for workers doing manual labor but for anyone interacting with the public. There were to be "no more extremes in clothing styles and color combinations…coordinated career clothes instill in fellow workers

The companies for which Work Wear Corporation made uniforms. (Charlotte R. Kramer, WRHS)

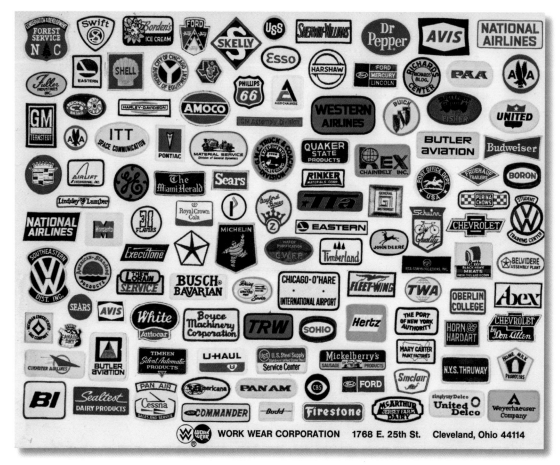

a unifying spirit."[10] Oleg Cassini, Bill Blass and Halston designed clothes for Work Wear. Companies like Avis made uniforms an important part of their brand. "If pressed," Leighton Rosenthal remarked, "we can even outfit Elizabethan barmaids."[11] In the 1960s Work Wear engaged the designer Barbara Dulian, whose goal was to be "the McDonald's of fashion."[12] She earned a special Coty Award, the equivalent to an Oscar in the fashion industry, for her first collection for Work Wear. Moving on from uniforms, Work Wear expanded in 1969 into disposable products as well, items that included caps and gloves in hospitals, for example. They even designed a bassinet and a waterproof operating room table sheet.[13] The firm's innovations ensured their continued success.

When the Frisch brothers returned from the war, they were eager to build their careers. Jerry Frisch was a born salesman. He encouraged his father to buy additional Raschel machines, because this would allow the company to be much more competitive. For many years after the war, the company specialized in multicolored T-shirts. Circular knitting machines, the company's next investment in technology, allowed them to make women's sweaters. These machines differed greatly from the Ketten-Stuhls and Raschel machines. As Marc Frisch described in his reminiscences,

> *Yarn cones were placed at the top and yarn fed through needles and the needle bed would turn making the stitch and feeding the yarn directed by its setup. Machines were of different gauges, fine and more coarse. We hired special knitter mecha ics who were able to engineer the machines. Some of the terms to describe the*

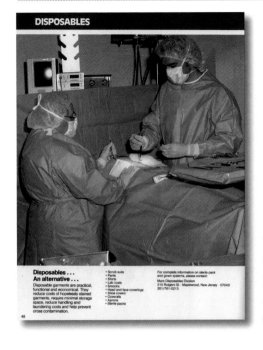

DISPOSABLES

Disposables . . .
An alternative . . .

Disposable garments are practical, functional and economical. They reduce costs of hopelessly stained garments, require minimal storage space, reduce handling and laundering costs and help prevent cross contamination.

• Scrub suits
• Pants
• Shirts
• Lab coats
• Smocks
• Head and face coverings
• Shoe covers
• Coveralls
• Aprons
• Sterile packs

For complete information on sterile pack and gown systems, please contact:
Mars Disposables Division
215 Rutgers St. · Maplewood, New Jersey 07040
201/761-0213

48

knitting machines would be Jersey, Jacquard, Double Jacquard. We also needed special finishing equipment for washing the fabric, steaming and pressing plus additional sewing machines for seaming, button holes and looping machines.[14]

The company was able to stay competitive and to innovate as necessary because of the technology behind the different machines. In the 1950s Frisch Knitting Mills reproduced a Belgian christening blanket. To make the blanket, they used the Ketten-Stuhl machines and then the Raschels for the fringe. "The Belgium Shawl" sold to stores selling clothing for infants and also in department stores like J. C. Penney. A move from Stanton Avenue to East 66th Street and Euclid enabled them to expand significantly.

Knitting mills continued to grow after the war, too. Leonard Rand took over Stone Knitting Mills from his father-in-law Harry Stone in 1947. By this time the firm had established a third mill in Winona, Minnesota, eventually taken over by Walker Woodworth's son, Leslie. After Harry Stone retired, Leonard Rand and Henry Rubin formed Ohio Knitting Mills. After graduating from the Philadelphia College of Textiles in 1967 and spending two years in New York in the apparel business, Gary, along with his wife Judy, returned to Cleveland to be a part of Ohio Knitting Mills. The company branched out to produce women's wear as well.

Ohio Knitting Mills made garments for other firms, putting in the labels of the other companies in clothes they had manufactured. Designed to operate in this way, the company did not have the prestige of turning out a product with a label that customers would associate with them. In addition, operating in this way meant a certain amount of risk. At times, companies did not pay for goods that they had ordered. Ohio Knitting Mills just had to take a loss. Similarly, there were no intellectual property rights on the design of a garment. Firms sometimes asked Ohio Knitting Mills to produce samples. The company would deliver the samples, but the potential customer would fail to come through with an order. Later, they would see that another manufacturer had been given the sample and copied their product. Regarding the theft of samples to steal patterns, Agnes Harichovszky of Ohio Knitting Mills commented, "that happened in a lot of cases."[15] Working with both suppliers and retailers, garment manufacturers took real risks.

In spite of these challenges, Ohio Knitting Mills survived into the twenty-first century, mostly because they adapted their older machines and processes to new designs. The firm had only two head designers over its nearly 80 years in business, first Sophie Ziskin

Work Wear made all kinds of uniforms for different working environments.
(Lois Wainwright, WRHS)

The Bobbie Brooks distribution center in 1968. (Sam Weisberg, Mrs. Shirley Kanner, and Mrs. Shirley Saltzman, WRHS)

Work Wear pioneered the concept of career clothes rental by focusing on fabric, style, and fit. They took their clothing into insurance companies and banks, white-collar fields not traditionally associated with uniforms. The idea of a "controlled appearance level" appealed to many business leaders. In a 1968 Newsday article, the headline trumpeted, "Now They're Packaging People".
(Lois Wainwright, WRHS)

Anniversary celebration,
Frisch Knitting Mills. O. N.
Fishel, back, center;
Norbert Hibshman, in
glasses looking at camera
bottom right; Leonard
Rand is to the left of
Hibshman. (Marc Frisch,
WRHS)

and then Elizabeth Foderaro. Foderaro, a West Side Italian descended from Sicilian immigrants, designed the pullovers, cardigans, and dresses that were sold to jobbers like Jack Winter, Bobbie Brooks, McGregor and Pendleton. These warp knitting machines enabled them to vary colors and textures. They made possible endless combinations that Foderaro could use in her designs for specific markets. The company used its original Raschel machines, but they also added other kinds of machines as they grew. The Philadelphia Jacquard machines they acquired in the 1940s to make durable fabrics for military purposes were turned to other, more fashionable uses. Circular machines created finer knits for the designs that

Florian Fashions, 1980s.
(Marc Frisch, WRHS)

required it, especially the Poor Boy, a short sleeve knit sweater that appealed to those wanting more colorful clothing after the war. Tom Rovas and Jules O'Hyde, the knitting machine engineers, were the unsung heroes of the company. Their work keeping the machines running enabled workers to realize Foderaro's designs and the company to deliver the product lines as promised. While products by French designers like Yves Saint Laurent sold for thousands of dollars, similar designs by Foderaro of Ohio Knitting Mills sold for less than thirty. The firm's technological innovations continued in later decades. Ohio Knitting Mills added new machines from Stoll Electronic in the 1980s and, in the 1990s, from Caperdoni, specialized machines that helped the company keep pace with the demanding changes of the marketplace. Ohio Knitting Mills was the only mill in the United States to have Caperdoni machines, which weaved and knitted at the same time. Such innovations helped the company last into the twenty-first century.

Clothing made in Cleveland was affordable and wearable by the average consumer. The experience of Campus Sweater and Sportswear, originally in operation in 1919 as Pontiac Knitting Mills (named after the General Motors brand),[16] confirms the utility of the clothing made in Cleveland. The founders of the company were Samuel S. Kaufman and Loren B. Weber. Weber was a former employee of Erie Dye. The company eventually developed 19 plants throughout the South, in addition to knitting mills in Pennsylvania and Indiana. Bernard Zuckerman, Vice President and Chief Engineer for Campus, designed many of these plants for the company during his 37 years of service. Zuckerman's children remember their father "in his white shirt and tie, sleeves rolled up, puffing on his pipe, standing at his drafting table producing engineering drawings of plants and additions he designed."[17]

Art Mayers attributed the company's initial success to copying. Mayers explained that they bought samples from

In the mid twentieth century hospital volunteers, usually young women, often wore red and white striped jumpers or smocks, thus earning them the title by which they became best known, "candy stripers". The distinctive red and white stripes signaled a friendly face. Hospital volunteers brought water or books and magazines to patients, assisted nurses, and helped out with other basic tasks. Work Wear provided uniforms that may have been worn by candy stripers across the country. (Charlotte R. Kramer, WRHS)

other companies and figured out how to make the same product for less.[18] Campus' major success was the Le Tigre brand of men's sportswear, including the polo shirt with the tiger as the logo, meant to compete with the Izod alligator. As Mayers said, "If MacGregor was the Cadillac of sportswear, Campus was the Chevrolet."[19] He echoed a slogan from the company's own advertising: "Campus makes it all – Campus makes fashion at prices that make sense."

Other firms, notably Bobbie Brooks and Dalton in women's wear, offered high- quality products priced to be affordable for the average consumer. Maurice Saltzman, the innovative leader behind Bobbie Brooks, grew up as an orphan in Bellefaire, the city's home for Jewish orphans since the 1860s and an institution to which he remained devoted his entire life. Saltzman's career is most certainly one of the greatest success stories in the garment industry.

Saltzman started at Lampl Fashions in 1934, when he was just 16 years old. At 17 he became the company's youngest traveling salesman, learning to drive on the byways of Alabama and Mississippi. When he returned to Cleveland, he was promoted to Assistant to the President of the company. Saltzman credited a natural instinct for knowing what the customer wanted for his rapid rise.

His instincts served him well. In 1939 he and Max Reiter, another Lampl salesman, decided to strike out on their own. Max Reiter was known as Rit and Saltzman as Morry, so they called their new company the Ritmor Sportswear Company, first located in the Bradley Building on West 6th Street. With start up capital of only $4,000, they began as jobbers working with contractors until they started to manufacture their own clothing line. The company began to grow. Saltzman and Reiter turned Ritmor into a multimillion-dollar business – in less than five years.

But it was the introduction of the Bobbie Brooks line for juniors that would transform the company. Bobbie Brooks, originally named Barbara Brooks after a friend, was forced to change its name due to prior usage of that name by another company. Bobbie was a "kicky" name and served Reiter and Saltzman well.[20] Saltzman described juniors as women who were a "little bit smaller, a little bit shorter, a little bit smaller busted and smaller hips". The idea was to sell clothes to young women who felt they were too old for the teen market but too young for the older fashions marketed to adult women. And if the clothing fit older women, too, that could only mean additional sales. Saltzman explained,

Young junior meant a girl from 13 to 18. But there was no age because a woman of 50 could have worn it if it fit her. But the idea was that this was a new field and that the young girl from the ages of 15 to 18 had no place in the store to go.

OHIO KNITTING MILLS 7500 STANTON

Garment industry support of Shaker Heights High School yearbook, 1968, Gary Rand and Cathy Federman. (Gary Rand, WRHS)

Saltzman's insight wasn't about how to make the product more cheaply or about some technological innovation. It was a marketing insight that, it turned out, he timed perfectly to coincide with the postwar baby boom and the rise of youth culture. The industry hailed Saltzman as "a scientific specialist in the youth market," the holy grail for garment manufacturers.[21] The juniors category transformed the industry. Retailers redesigned their space to market to this consumer group. The larger department stores created entire junior departments in which the coordinating Bobbie Brooks sets were featured.

Bobbie Brooks became one of the most recognizable names in fashion for young women. The company defined the junior audience as young women aged 14 to 24 and then refined the market to a younger cohort of 13 to 19 year olds. Bobbie Brooks specialized and then listened to its target audience, establishing a fashion board of teenagers from across the country to test their ideas and help them design their products. The most innovative feature of the Bobbie Brooks line was the coordinates, blouses, skirts, and other items that could be mixed and matched. This concept gave young women more choices and flexibility. Bobbie Brooks' reputation carried on into the 1980s, when John Cougar referenced them in his 1982 hit "Jack and Diane," a song about "two American kids growing up in the heartland":

> *Suckin' on a chili dog outside the Tastee Freez*
> *Diane's sittin' on Jackie's lap, he's got his hands between her knees*
> *Jackie say, Hey, Diane let's run off behind a shady tree*
> *Dribble off those Bobbie Brooks, let me do what I please*

Clothes made in Cleveland were instantly recognized throughout the nation.

Cover of the invitation to view the Dalton fall collection, 1989. (Marc Frisch, WRHS)

Max Reiter, left, and Maurice Saltzman celebrating the 10th anniversary of Ritmor Sportswear, 1949. (Janet Reiter Greenberg, WRHS)

Bobbie Brooks eventually established production facilities throughout the United States and abroad, but they kept their headquarters in Cleveland. The company took her name in 1960. The company's exponential growth did not negatively impact the importance of personal connections for those trying to get into the garment business. Throughout its existence, Bobbie Brooks provided opportunities to many who had a connection to Bellefaire. Cal Cohen, who worked his way up at Bobbie Brooks from a part-time job during college to the senior administration, recalled, "it was always said that you had to be a relative or somebody from Bellefaire" to get a job at Bobbie Brooks.[22]

The outstanding American athlete Babe Didrikson Zaharias endorsed the golf apparel of Cleveland's sportswear firm, Serbin, Inc. Founded in Cleveland in 1943 by Lewis I. Serbin and M. John Serbin, the company manufactured women's clothing, including dresses and sportswear. Serbin and L. N. Gross shared a plant in Fayetteville, Tennessee, from 1948 to 1949. In 1951 the Serbin family and company relocated to Miami, where the company operated under various names until 1991. From 1953 to 1957 the family sponsored the Serbin Open, a tournament on the LPGA tour. Babe Zaharias won the tournament in 1955. (Robert J. Kahn, WRHS)

In 1949, Saltzman and Arthur Dery of Excelsior teamed up to establish the Fine Gauge Knitwear Company focusing on making cashmere sweaters. Saltzman had already established Ritmor with Reiter. The Fine Gauge Knitwear Company began making sweaters, and the company became known for having produced the first white cashmere sweater. This sweater helped to establish what came to be known as the Dalton line. The company soon changed its name to Dalton to capitalize on its most popular line. The company intentionally played off the Royal Doulton name, which had a reputation for fine china and fine living. Dery bought out Saltzman in 1957. Brothers Ken, James, and Robert Dery helped their father run the business. Ken Dery explained why their products, which were priced just slightly higher than others, sold so well. According to Dery, "People might not be able to buy a Mercedes, but they could buy a Dalton sweater set."[23] Again, Cleveland manufacturers were making clothing that people both wanted and could afford.

The move of Phoenix Dye from Chicago to Cleveland signaled most clearly the success of the industry in the city at mid-century. The industry relied on its suppliers. When Erie Dye and Processing went out of business, it left Cleveland's knitwear manufacturers without a local dye house. Erie Dye and Processing Company, run by the Haber family, supplied dyed yarn to firms in Cleveland. The Habers capitalized on the growing market for knitgoods produced in Cleveland. Located on East 55th Street, the company employed Rudy Adler, a chemist who developed a special dehairing process for dehaired cashmere and camel hair. His process helped the company break the monopoly the Scots had on cashmere sweaters and to transition from being a supplier to being both a supplier and manufacturer.

Erie Dye formed the Cashmere Corporation of America to supply the cashmere, camel, and lambswool yarns to domestic knitters. The company, run by Richard L. Haber, wanted to make and market the final product, too, and so they formed another corporation, Hadley. Hadley sweaters were popular among the youth of the 50s and 60s. Erie Dye had transformed itself into the world's only completely vertical cashmere firm in the world, going from unscoured raw goat hair to finished sweaters. Unfortunately, the company could not sustain this business model for very long. Erie Dye was sold to the Arsham brothers in 1957 and Hadley (formerly the Cashmere Corporation of America) was acquired by Dalton.

Cleveland's knitting mills had been using Chicago's Phoenix Dye for much of their work already, and Phoenix, founded by a family of German immigrants, the Susens, was looking to expand. Cleveland's manufacturers took advantage of the coincidence and successfully encouraged Phoenix Dye to come to Cleveland. This well-established firm contributed much to the industry in the city. The move resulted from the efforts of the Cleveland group of the National Knitted Outerwear Association. The business leaders recognized the opportunity to move a significant business to the area. They investigated the options and encouraged the firm to come to Cleveland. Such foresight was responsible for new jobs for Clevelanders and for the continued success of the industry overall.

In 1960 Joseph & Feiss offered a short sleeve suit for men at B. Altman and Co. in New York. The suit sold for $45. Matching Bermuda shorts were extra. Richard Adler, then president of Joseph & Feiss, suggested that the company might offer the suit at other retailers if there were enough interest. Short sleeve suits still haven't caught on.

there
she is
again...
in a
Dalton

Superlative pantsuit in pure 100% wool double knit. Sizes 6 to 16, about $150. Prices slightly higher in the West. Dalton of America, New York City or Willoughby, Ohio. Also makers of James Kenrob Sportswear.

Advertisement for Dalton, 1970s. (Arthur, Ken, Jim, and Bob Dery, WRHS)

American fashion designer Halston appeared in a Work Wear catalog featuring a collection of his designs, 1979. (Charlotte R. Kramer, WRHS)

The apparel industry flourished after World War II, just like other sectors of the economy. The industry in these years was the fulfillment of the American Dream. Success, however, did not mean the industry had become less challenging. Richard Adler's concern as chief executive of Joseph & Feiss and as head of the Clothing Manufacturers Association in the late 1960s was the same as that of Louis N. Gross in the first decades of the twentieth century – how to respond to changes in the market. Adler was called a man of four seasons because he advocated working in four seasons throughout the year to maximize profit-making opportunities. Like other successful garment manufacturers, he recognized that fashion changed quickly, and that his firm had to offer lines that appealed to customers with changing tastes. As head of the nationwide Clothing Manufacturers Association he made an effort to lead his field to adopt common policies. Though his term as president was widely regarded a success, unity among clothing manufacturers was nearly impossible to achieve, as he himself admitted. For example, the tradition of Market Week, when manufacturers would begin the selling of their product to retailers, was something of a relic in the late 1960s. In 1970 the peak of manufacturers selling to retailers was two weeks before the opening of Market Week. The seasons had shortened. Manufacturers now had to prepare for seasons that were much shorter in length, meaning they had to change their offerings more often. Indeed, Richard Adler was right. They went in and out of business every six months.

Rayon was just one of the synthetic fibers available to manufacturers in mid-twentieth century Cleveland. Industrial Rayon Corporation prospered in Cleveland's West Boulevard neighborhood until 1938, when it moved to Painesville. In addition to being used in garments, rayon was also used in automotive products during **World War II.** (Special Collections, Michael Schwartz Library, Cleveland State University)

"Here you had a group of

more humane employers."

SAM JANIS SERVED AS CLEVELAND'S REGIONAL DIRECTOR OF THE ILGWU, 1963 - 1978. He arrived in Cleveland decades after the unions had taken hold, but he was uniquely placed to observe conflict between employers and their employees. He delivered this assessment of the Cleveland garment manufacturers in an oral history interview in the 1980s. Despite the fact he was a union man, his experiences had shown him that cooperation between groups with opposing interests was indeed possible and, in Cleveland, easier to achieve than elsewhere. The cost of labor was an important factor in the decline of the industry in Cleveland, but it was not the only one. Cleveland's garment manufacturers achieved some real success in the good years of the 1960s and 1970s. But the circumstances that had caused the industry to grow had changed significantly, and the industry's successful days were numbered.

Tower Press Building, originally home to H. Black and Company, 2013. (Cindy Bruml)

Too Many Pink Sweaters

NDIVIDUAL COMPANIES FOLDED FOR A NUMBER OF REASONS. Some manufacturers got out of the business because of union influence. Others simply failed to stay relevant as fashions changed. Still other families raised children who moved on to other endeavors and left the family business. But the late twentieth century decline in the industry was nationwide.

The decline occurred later than one might think. Nationwide, employment in the industry peaked in 1973. Production reached its highest level in 1987. Both economists and those in the industry agree that the rise in imports explains the decline. Imports accounted for 5.2 percent of consumption in 1970. By 1988 that percentage increased to 26.1 percent.[1] Production in Asia increased for the same reasons the industry took off among U.S. immigrants in the late nineteenth century. In addition, trade agreements opened up products from China and elsewhere. Raw materials were common and it did not take much capital to set up business. The pattern of the industry simply repeated itself. Significantly, U.S. government policy of the 1990s, especially the North American Free Trade Agreement (NAFTA), encouraged free trade and did not protect the garment industry from imports. According to Fred Jones, who owned Phoenix Dye with his father, NAFTA was a silver bullet that killed domestic production.[2] NAFTA disadvantaged the local producers. After NAFTA, the textile mills that justified the move of Phoenix Dye to Cleveland in the 1950s were just no longer there. Phoenix Dye was liquidated in 1998. An industry with a long and proud history in the U.S. declined precipitously.

Of Cleveland's more established firms from the nineteenth century, Richman Brothers was one of the most successful in the postwar period. Nathan G. Richman was the last of the brothers to die, in 1941, but the company continued to prosper under the leadership of a nephew, Richard Kohn, and then a cousin of the founders, George Richman. George Richman turned the company into the nation's largest clothing chain in the 1950s, with 119 retail outlets. The company also acquired the Stein stores, a Southern chain, and established the Adam's Row stores to sell trendier fashions. But the family's influence on the company did not last much longer. New York's F. W. Woolworth Co. acquired Richman Brothers in 1969. The firm ceased to be profitable in 1992, and Woolworth shut down all of the company's operations in the Cleveland area. Remarkably, the Richman Brothers Foundation continues to aid retirees of the company and make other charitable contributions. Shea Kui Ng and Derek Ng, father and son investors from Hong Kong and immigrants to Cleveland, bought the once state-of-the-art facility on East 55th Street in 2009.

Joseph & Feiss operated profitably for decades after World War II. Felix S. Mayer served as president of Joseph & Feiss from 1931 to 1957 and oversaw the firm's greatest period of expansion. For many of the years of his tenure he served simultaneously as president of Michaels, Stern & Co. in Rochester, New York. The amenities that had once been enjoyed by employees now served other purposes. The theater, bowling alley, and swimming pool were converted to warehousing. Workers hauled suits around on the floor of the swimming pool.[3] A space that once offered workers relief from the heat became a worksite.

Mayer planned for his succession well when he chose Richard Adler of Rochester to come to Joseph & Feiss

Shopping for a suit, Richman Brothers store in Cleveland, 1950s. (Robert Harger, WRHS)

We wish you a Happy Day every day through-out the Year

THE H. BLACK CO.
DESIGNERS AND MAKERS
PARIS - CLEVELAND

THE WOOLTEX FACTORY
DURING THE BLIZZARD OF NOV. 10TH 1913

Advertisement,
The H. Black Co.
(WRHS)

as president. Like many executives at his level, Adler commuted between Cleveland and New York City, spending much of his time away from his family.[4] Adler planned to sell Joseph & Feiss with Dan Loeser of Cleveland's Hahn Loeser, longtime attorneys for the firm. Chicago's Hart Schaffner Marx was the preferred buyer but Phillips-Van Heusen was seeking to expand.[5] Phillips-Van Heusen was a more appropriate match, and so Joseph & Feiss merged with the firm in 1966. However, conflict between the Phillips family and Adler, in the limelight as president of the Clothing Manufacturers Association, eventually resulted in Adler leaving the company before the natural end of his career. Other executives from Joseph & Feiss eventually bought the firm back from Van Heusen before selling to Hugo Boss AG, a West German firm, in 1989. The company still had 800 employees in 1995, but in 1997, the plant on West 53rd was closed and manufacturing transferred to a distribution center on Tiedeman Road. Spanish, Romanian, Chinese and Vietnamese were just some of the languages spoken by the 300 workers employed by Hugo Boss in the early 2000s. When Hugo Boss attempted to close the plant in 2009, a high-profile union campaign, involving the participation of actor Danny Glover, succeeded in keeping the factory open.[6] In March 2015 Hugo Boss announced plans to sell the plant to W. Diamond Group Corp., a manufacturer of men's suits for Hart Schaffner Marx.

After being bought out by Maurice Saltzman, Max Reiter went on to produce clothing under other labels, including Karen Sue. In 1954, Reiter purchased Printz-Biederman. When ILGWU leader Sam Janis assessed the garment industry in mid 1960s Cleveland, he noted that Printz-Biederman, once the area's largest manufacturer of ladies coats, had already been sold and that there were two companies that showed continued growth, Bobbie Brooks and Dalton.[7] Printz-Biederman, once a model of industrial democracy, suffered significant losses throughout the 1960s and 1970s and eventually closed in 1978. Sidney Walzer, who spent his career making women's clothing and much of that time at Printz-Biederman, concluded that Printz-Biederman closed in part because they did not keep up with the fashion of the times:

> *….business dropped off, and they did not keep up with the style situation. Season after season they kept on manufacturing the same type of staple sort of garment, not directed at the young girls, but mostly toward middle-aged women. It was not the most fashionable, and this was why their business dropped off.*[8]

Exterior photo of Joseph & Feiss, West 53rd Street, 2014. (Cindy Bruml, WRHS)

The 1960s and 1970s were still pretty good years for the garment industry and especially for Bobbie Brooks and Dalton in particular, but technological changes and increased competition from abroad began to take a significant toll. Most of those involved in the industry attribute the decline to the use of cheap labor first in the American South and then overseas. Garments imported from abroad were just as good in quality as those produced in the United States. American garment companies could not compete with the lower labor costs abroad and, because of older equipment, could not compete on quality either. As Mike Klein, an executive with M and D Simon for many years, put it, "At some point, value added doesn't matter, it's all price."[9] Buzz Rosenfeld, a Cleveland labor attorney, echoed his point, "People just don't want to pay more than somebody else."[10]

The fate of Frisch Knitting Mills was tied closely to the organization of its workers. Frisch had been making sweaters for Bobbie Brooks for some time when a new union contract at Bobbie Brooks required it to work only with unionized shops. Bobbie Brooks encouraged Frisch to join the ILGWU. Frisch had never been unionized, but its wages were above union scale. Though in the same location as Stone Knitting Mills, Frisch had not been a part of the 1937 strike. According to Marc Frisch, neither management nor labor wanted to join the union. As a result, Bobbie Brooks cancelled its orders, delivering a crushing blow to Frisch.

Garland, a Bobbie Brooks competitor based in Massachusetts, came to Frisch's rescue. Garland's sweaters were a higher quality product than those made by Bobbie Brooks, requiring Frisch employees to learn additional skills. The effort paid off, and Frisch soon had to acquire new knitting machines. The instability of the garment industry, however, had taken its toll on the Frisch brothers. Marc accepted an offer to join Bobbie Brooks in 1967, beginning a related but separate career in the field. His brother Jerry eventually sold Frisch to Bobbie Brooks. Marc began traveling between

delectable collectibles....mmmm!

Florian Fashions, 1980s.
(Marc Frisch, WRHS)

Cleveland and New York, overseeing yarn production and eventually working with the Bobbie Brooks plant in Ponce, Puerto Rico, and later in Asia.

Cal Cohen, an executive with Bobbie Brooks from the early fifties to the late eighties, attributed the decline of Bobbie Brooks to the collapse of double knits in the 1976-1977 season. The popularity of double knit took the industry by storm, but it didn't last. According to Cohen, customers eventually realized they were simply wearing plastic and they demanded natural fibers once again. Cohen estimated Bobbie Brooks lost tens of millions of dollars exiting the double-knit business. The reversion to other fibers resulted in huge losses on expensive machinery that could not be used to make other products. Investing so heavily in double knits betrayed the main principle of the industry – you have to be nimble and be able to react quickly to changes in fashion.

Additional losses in other ventures and investments by Bobbie Brooks were enough to weaken the company to the point of bankruptcy, declared in 1982. Cohen also suggests that the lack of a succession plan at Bobbie Brooks, a plan to replace Saltzman, also hurt the company at the time of its crisis in the early 1980s. None of Saltzman's three daughters or their spouses was interested in developing the business further, and there was no natural successor among the top leadership. Because of Saltzman's high moral standards, Bobbie Brooks tried to reorganize in bankruptcy agreeing to pay 100 percent of its obligations over time. That plan left the company financially weak leading Bobbie Brooks to the brink of bankruptcy again in 1985. Pubco Corporation, a company primarily in commercial printing that had acquired a small department store chain, acquired control of Bobbie Brooks. Robert H. Kanner led the company at the time. Realizing that garment manufacturing was not likely to return to profitability, Pubco caused Bobbie Brooks to license its name, which returned Bobbie Brooks to profitability. Dollar General Stores contracted to offer Bobbie Brooks exclusively in 2005 and launched the Bobbie Brooks line in its stores in 2010, as part of the company's strategy to move into the retail space occupied by Walmart.[11]

Florian Fashions may have been the youngest of the larger manufacturers to succeed in the postwar decades. Founded by the Cleveland-born Jerome Lurie in 1959, Florian Fashions made dresses in both petite and large sizes. Its lines Jerrie Lurie, Kevin Stuart Petite, Mynette, and Jessica, Ltd all took their names from various family members. Jerrie Lurie was an old-fashioned salesman. A colorful figure, he had worked as a comedian in the Catskills. Lurie designed his own dresses and sold them directly to merchants. Florian Fashions succeeded in cooperation with Gottfried Dress Company. Entering a deal to share the Gottfried sales force, Lurie eventually bought the company, afraid that Gottfried might go out of business. In the late 1970s Jerrie Lurie entered the sportswear market, working with others in the industry to produce new designs.

Marc Frisch, left, and Gregg Lurie, in Taiwan, 1970s. Frisch continued to work in the garment industry after the closure of his family firm, working with companies in Asia that provided materials to companies in Cleveland. Frisch's company, FLOMAR, made garments for Jerry Lurie labels, including Jessica Ltd. and Kevin Stuart and for the Dalton label, which had been bought by Jerry Lurie. (Marc Frisch, WRHS)

FROM NINETEENTH CENTURY OVERALLS TO TWENTY-FIRST CENTURY CLEANROOMS

The oldest garment manufacturing company still in operation in Northeast Ohio is Euclid Vidaro Manufacturing Company. It began with a pair of brothers who came to Cleveland in the 1870s and started making work shirts. Today the grandson of one of those brothers continues the company's work, specializing in clothing and accessories used in cleanroom environments.

Brothers Simon and David Rosenblatt most likely came to the United States in the 1850s. David Rosenblatt was wounded in the First Battle of Bull Run. It is not known when they came to Cleveland, but they founded Rosenblatt Brothers in 1870. The company was located in the heart of downtown Cleveland at 28 Broadway. Around 1900 they expanded into overalls, jeans and work jackets. The company suffered during the Great Depression but remained within the family.

During World War II, Euclid Manufacturing, as the company was then known, made women's coveralls for defense plants. After relocating to Kent in 1952, the company expanded significantly throughout the next decades. Charles B. Rosenblatt, grandson of Simon and great-nephew of David, has run the business since 1959. In 2008 the company was renamed Euclid Vidaro, after the initials of Henry Vircant and Ed Davis, partners in the business since the 1960s, and Rosenblatt.

Today the company makes a range of specialized items for the aerospace, medical and pharmaceutical industries, including coveralls, lab coats, and boots and shoe covers. These industries need materials that can be used in environments that must be kept as sterile as possible.

This part of the garment industry is high tech. The twenty-first century workspace of Euclid Vidaro is far-removed from our image of men and women bustling about on the cutting-room floor of a factory at the turn of the twentieth century. The processes for making the garment remain the same: design, cutting, sewing and finishing. But this time the fabric may include filaments of stainless steel and conduct electricity. Such garments help workers in the electronics industry stay comfortable. The Rosenblatt family has developed a niche in the industry that has led it to remain in business for more than 144 years. Charles B. Rosenblatt and Euclid Vidaro, 2010. (Marc Frisch)

There were still some good years left in the industry when Ron Gottfried of Gottfried Dress Company met Jerrie Lurie of Florian Fashions in the late 1970s. Their businesses complemented each other. Gottfried made women's dresses in special sizes, and Florian made regular sizes. They arranged to share the physical plant and Gottfried offered Florian its sales force.

According to Gottfried, "Everyone won. Our volumes exploded, our factories were humming, and our sales staff was ecstatic. We would get literally piles of orders from the shows. We would throw them on the floor and DANCE on them, laughing with glee." Gregg Lurie of Florian Fashions. (Bob Mendes, WRHS)

In the 1970s Jerome Lurie's sons, older brother Gregg and twins Keith and Ken, were about a generation younger than many of their peers in the industry. When Dalton ceased operations in 1987, they were well placed to redesign the line and move the company forward. They streamlined their operations when they took over Dalton. They stopped knitting their own fabrics and discontinued one of their own labels. Florian made their blazers, shorts and shirts in Cleveland, Canton and New York State. They placed representatives in several cities throughout the United States to market their products.

Jerrie Lurie died in 1985, just before his sons acquired Dalton. Dalton offered the brothers a chance to continue the company's success. Florian struggled with the union in the 1980s and 1990s. Jerrie Lurie had taken the attitude that you can't fight the union. After his father's death, Gregg Lurie fought, somewhat successfully. He refused to sign a new contract and the workers went on strike. Gregg Lurie had already arranged for production to continue in South Carolina. The workers then came back after renegotiations. Florian Fashions produced a line under the Dalton label until 2000.

Other firms held on until the mid-1980s. An outside investment group took control of L. N. Gross in 1984 and changed the name to Bradley Sportswear, Inc. Work Wear was bedeviled by its own success. The company was charged with controlling the manufacture of industrial garments under the Clayton Antitrust Act in 1968. As a result, the company sold

The building that housed Excelsior Knitting Mills, Euclid Sportswear (fifth floor), and Frisch Knitting Mills (fourth floor) on Euclid Avenue at East 66th Street, Dunham Tavern Museum in the lower right. The building originally housed Lake City Sales and stored automobiles. Torn down in 2012. (Marc Frisch, WRHS)

off its industrial laundries in 1977 and reorganized. At the same time, the company incorporated ARA Services to operate its rental business. The company ceased making clothes in Cleveland in 1984. Paine Webber Capital of New York acquired Work Wear in 1986. Paine Webber sold off the European divisions of Work Wear and moved all operations to Greensboro, North Carolina. Work Wear's Buckeye Garment Rental on East 93rd Street is now Aramark, the international concern that provides uniforms to hospitals, businesses, stadiums and arenas.

Ohio Knitting Mills managed to make it through the 70s and 80s by designing popular products. Taking off on the popularity of Central and South America among the counterculture of the late 60s and early 70s, Elizabeth Foderaro designed a poncho that was colorful and versatile and appealing to girls and women around the country. The versatility of the company enabled it to survive the ebbs and flows of the industry. The company was still making men's sweaters at the same time. They made over a million ribbed mock turtlenecks for Pendleton in 1980, business that was crucial to their continued success throughout the 90s. By the early 2000s, SASA, a real estate holding company owned by the Rand family, had purchased all of the land surrounding the Ohio Knitting Mills location at East 61st

An editorial published in The Plain Dealer on April 5, 1933, neatly summarized what happens to wages when customers insist on the lowest prices:

The Plain Dealer's study of how Cleveland wages in many lines have hit a bottom far below subsistence levels is a sharp reminder that the worker is often as badly off as the workless in these distressing times. Nor is the modern "sweatshop" confined to the garment and needle trades in which it flourished in its old form 20 years ago. Today's victims include the household drudge whose mistress boasts at the bridge table of how she gets her domestic help for little or nothing.

The picture is one in part of greed and selfishness exploiting the opportunity handed it by the Depression, but in larger degree, we believe it is due to cutthroat competition, encouraged by the readiness of the buying public to be lured by price rather than quality. Even this, however, is not a wholly satisfactory explanation, when it is evident that a 100 percent increase for some of these ruthlessly underpaid workers would add only a few cents to the price of a finished garment.

Such wages, of course, are obviously unsocial. They add to the burden of public charity and by pushing the purchasing power of the workers down to virtually nothing, prevent business recovery.

As Mrs. Franklin D. Roosevelt points out in her appeal to American women, a partial remedy lies with the shopper who will insist upon assurance against sweatshop goods. "No sweatshop Easter" is a slogan to which all socially minded women should rally. If they will do so emphatically enough some of these desperate conditions may be corrected.

Workers in coat department on sewing floor of Joseph & Feiss, 1932.
(Joseph & Feiss Company, WRHS)

Street. This land was then bought by the city of Cleveland with the idea that a medical technology center would be built on the 18 acres of land that the Rand family had acquired. After a temporary move to Willoughby, Gary Rand decided after three years that it was in the best interest of everybody to close the Ohio Knitting Mills operation. He then entered an agreement with local sculptor Steve Tatar to sell the vintage sweaters of Ohio Knitting Mills and Stone Knitting Mills.[12]

Among those who worked in the garment industry the most often mentioned reason for the decline of the industry in the area is foreign imports. At least one leader in the industry, Stephen C. Lampl, attributes the decline of his family firm to the influence of organized labor. Lampl made the decision to sell out to Bobbie Brooks in the late 1960s because he could not compete with the Bobbie Brooks plants in the South, which worked with non-union labor.[13] In an earlier period, Federal Knitting Mills and S. Korach Co. attributed their closures to difficulties with labor.

Organized labor certainly transformed the industry, but the success of firms like Bobbie Brooks and Dalton so late in the twentieth century suggests that the union did not keep manufacturers from making significant profits. Sam Janis summarized his view of the employers in Cleveland:

Here you had a more humane group of employers. Occasionally you would get a chiseller; but, basically, they were this much higher than the employer in the large city. The union and the industry, industry by the way is very sensitive in the sense that they have a lot of feeling for people; it is a people industry. It is not like the automobile industry where you have a very heavy capital investment in equipment and machines, here, you have the investment in basically people…The garment industry is…dealing with labor intensive with people. The employers of the industry that still prevail in many different parts of the country were immigrants themselves. They knew, they worked their way up, they didn't come in rich. They worked their

Lion Knitting Mills, run by the Hibshman families, ceased operations in 1990, after 78 years in business. Seth M. Bodner, noted in Knitting Times,
It is too soon to know whether the demise of Lion will register on the seismographs of the U. S. International Trade Commission as a relevant factor in determining whether dumped man-made fiber sweaters are hurting the domestic sweater industry, but anyone in the market knows that the massive presence of cheap man-made fiber sweaters from Korea, Taiwan and Hong Kong has hurt the entire market and every firm in it, be they specialists in cotton goods, wool goods, man-made fiber goods or producers of all of them. Site of Lion Knitting Mills, 3256 West 25th Street. (Cleveland City Planning Commission)

way up where they are the employers now. They have a feeling for the people. So they aren't that callous, so that they want a free society that says… 'we don't want people to have a blue card to come to America. We came to America, our parents came to America. They made something here; they had an opportunity. We want those people to come here too. There is room in America for all these people'…They would rather have an industry that is well policed, where everything is working properly.[14]

Sam Janis also asserted that during his tenure as the regional union leader from 1964 to 1978 no manufacturers left Cleveland for non-union labor.

The view of Ron Gottfried, who was with both L. N. Gross and his own Gottfried Dress Company, concurs with Janis' assessment of the relationship between labor and management:

I joined the group who said that the demise of the fashion industry in Cleveland has no bearing whatsoever to do, or you can't lay the blame at the feet of the union people, in my opinion. I think they have recognized that this has been a shrinking market for them. I think, at least in my dealings in two companies, they have been very realistic and very cooperative. I almost think to a surprising degree. I think they're very enlightened. I think that's an easy way out for a lot of people to shift the blame for their own lack of management abilities or their own lack of marketing abilities because almost everybody in our industry has to live with the same thing.[15]

But other factors must also be taken into account. Family-owned companies also experienced significant difficulties transitioning from one generation to the next, and not all made that transition successfully. Some firms may have lasted somewhat longer with different or more effective leadership, however difficult the challenges from market forces. Gregg Lurie suggested that the decline of specialty stores in light of the growth of big box stores played a role in the decline of the industry. In addition, the decline of the garment industry was simply a part of the decline of manufacturing in the United States and the nation's transition to a service economy. After many decades, the garment industry in the region simply succumbed to the changes in the market and to changes in fashion. Regarding the changeability of the market, Cal Cohen remembers Maurice Saltzman saying humorously, "A policeman in Kansas City blows a whistle and says this color is dead."[16] Similarly, Saltzman's colleague David Reinthal remarked,

The H. Black Co. building, **2014.** (Cindy Bruml, WRHS)

In the sweater business, if something becomes good, you have to move very fast. We had a thing back in about he fifties. Men's pink sweaters became very popular, and suddenly about one third of our production was on men's pink sweaters. And for about two or three months it was the hottest thing in the world. We couldn't make enough of them. And then suddenly somebody took a knife and chopped it off and nobody wanted pink sweaters any more, and then we got stuck with maybe a thousand, two thousand dozen men's pink sweaters, which you couldn't sell at fifty cents a piece.[17]

Change was the only constant. Sometimes it favored the entrepreneur, sometimes it did not. The growth of ready-to-wear and the start of mass production in the early twentieth century transformed the manufacture of clothing. Yet as skirts became shorter and suit jackets more plaid, one thing stayed the same: the need to sell. And that meant constant monitoring of trends and innovative changes in styles and production. Cleveland's garment manufacturers managed successfully for decades, but, in the end, they were not able to innovate enough to compete with foreign manufacturers. Sometimes there were just too many pink sweaters.

Joseph & Feiss factory on West 53rd, 2013. (Cindy Bruml, WRHS)

A colorful mural by local enamelist Kenneth Bates greeted visitors to the new Campus Sportswear building at 3955 Euclid Ave. The large mural, visible from the street, featured team pennants and images of a football player, a tennis player, a basketball going through a hoop, boating and other sports. The mural depicted the work of the company in 1956. Started as Pontiac Knitting Mills in Cleveland in 1922, the company was acquired in 1964 by Interco, a clothing, shoe and discount store conglomerate. The Campus division retained some authority but its Cleveland headquarters was closed in 1982, shortly after the deaths of the company's founders, Loren Bertram Weber, in 1978, and Samuel Kaufman, in 1980.

Campus Sportswear mural (The Walter Leedy Postcard Collection, Special Collections, Michael Schwartz Library, Cleveland State University)

CONCLUSION

THE INFLUENCE OF THE GARMENT INDUSTRY ON TODAY'S CITY IS EASY TO MISS. Many factories stand forlorn, in ruins, with little sign that they once employed thousands. The flag no longer flies outside the shell of the building that housed Richman Brothers on East 55th Street. The home to so many Slovenian workers has become a hulking reminder of the city's industrial past. The buildings that made up Joseph & Feiss on West 53rd Street are covered with ivy and graffiti. Paths through the brush, strewn with garbage, lead up and into the building itself. The National Screw building on Stanton Avenue, the home to knitting mills, is completely gone. Stanton Avenue simply ends in a grove of trees, proof that the very landscape of the city is changing. The owners and workers left long ago for the suburbs and other opportunities. Their descendants often have only a vague notion about how their ancestors made a living.

Like the buildings we often drive past without a second thought, Cleveland's contribution to fashion is easily overlooked, too. Steve Tatar's pop-up shops for Ohio Knitting Mills are one of the most visible signs of the industry left in Cleveland. Other significant aspects of the legacy of the garment industry are harder to detect but perhaps more important. When asked about the influence of the garment industry on the city, Bart Simon, from the family firm of M and D Simon, commented simply, "These were the people who gave to the Federation."[1] These comments summarize the effect of the industry on the city since the early twentieth century. The philanthropy of garment industry entrepreneurs began with the first companies founded in the 1840s and goes back to one of Cleveland's first Jewish families. Like George Davis and Benjamin Peixotto, later leaders in the industry established and led organizations that became central to the welfare of the community. Tom Adler, the son of Joseph & Feiss' Richard Adler, echoed Bart Simon's remark, saying that, without the success of the garment industry, "A lot of money would not be here to support the Jewish and general community."[2]

Men like Charles Eisenman and John Anisfield became significant leaders in the community within just a few decades of the establishment of the industry in Cleveland. The philanthropy championed by these men with the establishment of the Federation of Jewish Welfare Charities in 1903 continues, not least because of the mid-twentieth century success of the garment industry. Samuel Rosenthal used his wealth from making overalls to support Jewish education at all levels; his son Leighton nobly continued his work and his philanthropy, including commitments to Park Synagogue and Case Western Reserve University. Maurice Saltzman never forgot his roots as an orphan in Bellefaire; he became a model of community leadership. When Richard Adler left Joseph & Feiss, he began a life in public service as head of the Greater Cleveland Growth Association, making concrete the connection between the garment industry and the growth of the region. Even the work of the early manufacturer John Anisfield resonates today. The Anisfield-Wolf Book Awards, established by his daughter Edith Anisfield Wolf, honor his commitment to social justice by bestowing annual awards on books that address issues of racism and diversity.

The workers themselves are a no less important legacy of the industry. Making dresses, cloaks, suits and sweaters enabled them to buy homes, feed their families, send children to school and live comfortably in retirement. Work in the garment industry offered them a chance to learn skills and eventually find jobs elsewhere. Work side by side with others from so many different backgrounds also facilitated the assimilation of the immigrant and better relations between blacks and whites. Many of the former employees of these companies have fond memories of their decades at work. Tensions between workers and employers were comparatively calm. The parties and picnics created a community environment. The community of the workplace was perhaps especially important, and strong, in the 1910s and 1920s, when recent immigrants found themselves in a strange new world. But the parties went on into the 1950s and 1960s. In 2012 Jennie Miklic Turk recalled her days as a Richman Brothers employee decades earlier.[3] She described the advantages of working for Richman Brothers:

> *Three brothers owned Richman Brothers. When I was 16, I went to work for Richman Brothers. I did not have a mother or father here, and they gave me a job and I was only 16. I did not know how to speak English but they had a translator that could help me. I want to say how very good they were. Every morning they greeted us at the door. We started working at 8:00 A.M. We had cooks that made hot meals for us for 3 cents to 50 cents. We had a doctor and a nurse in the office for 9 hours. We had one hour for lunch. Every Wednesday we had live music for one hour. We also had a place where we could worship. We got paid every Friday and we got cash money. Every birthday we got a gift, when we got married we got a gift and when we had a wedding shower or a baby shower they paid us for a whole day so we could say thank you to our friends. Also every pay they gave us something extra added to our pay. When it was very hot they gave us soft drinks. There was also a picnic (Euclid Beach Park) where they chose Miss Richman Brothers. There was ballroom dancing that day and we had rides for the whole day.*

> *I am very grateful for all they did for me. If there is a heaven, they should be there.*

The workplace was not solely a place of labor and routine. It was also a place where workers made friends and socialized and, in some sense, found a home for their labor. Somehow it seems appropriate that the purpose of the city's most successful garment manufacturing firm was "to clothe people for work".[4] The immigrants came to work, and making clothes changed people's lives. The need for clothes gave immigrants opportunities. From peddling to manufacturing to selling, immigrants seized those opportunities and built new lives as Americans.

Endnotes

Introduction

1. MS. 5032 United National Clothing Collection, Greater Cleveland Branch Records, 1945-1946, Western Reserve Historical Society (WRHS).
2. Bryner, *The Garment Trades* (Cleveland: The Survey Committee of the Cleveland Foundation, 1916), 19.
3. U. S. Census, 1890, 1910.
4. MS. 5106 Stanley Garfinkel Oral History Collection, Container 1, Folder 24, WRHS.
5. See the exhibit catalog, *A Perfect Fit: The Garment Industry and American Jewry* (New York: Yeshiva University Museum, 2005).

From Village to City

1. "Fifty Years Ago", I. Joseph, MS 3886 Joseph & Feiss Company Records, Container 1, Folder 1, WRHS.
2. Stanley Garfinkel, "Garment Industry", *The Encyclopedia of Cleveland History*, http://ech.case.edu/cgi/article.pl?id=GI, accessed November 28, 2013.
3. For an explanation of the argument that the garment industry contributed significantly to the material success of the Jewish community in the United States, see Adam D. Mendelsohn, *The Rag Race: How Jews Sewed their Way to Success in America and the British Empire* (New York: New York University Press, 2015).
4. Phyllis Dillon and Andrew Godley, "The Evolution of the Jewish Garment Industry, 1840-1940," *Chosen Capital: The Jewish Encounter with American Capitalism*, ed. Rebecca Kobrin (New Brunswick, New Jersey: Rutgers University Press, 2012), 56.
5. Green, Nancy L. *Ready-to-Wear and Ready-to-Work: A Century of Industry and Immigrants in Paris and New York* (Durham: Duke University Press, 1997), 217.
6. Andrew Godley, "Jewish Immigrants and the Garment Industry: A View from London," *A Perfect Fit: The Garment Industry and American Jewry*, 1860-1960, eds. Gabriel M. Goldstein and Elizabeth E. Greenberg (Lubbock, Texas: Texas Tech University Press for Yeshiva University Museum, 2012), 20-21.
7. Mendelsohn, *The Rag Race*, 217. A survey of Jewish economic activity published in *Fortune* in 1936 showed that Jews made up 4 per cent of the country's population in 1936 but 85 percent of the participants in the production of men's clothing and 95 per cent in the production of women's clothing. Editors of *Fortune*, *Jews in America* (New York: Random House, 1936), 49; William M. Kephart, "What is the Position of Jewish Economy in the United States", *Social Forces* 28 (December 1949): 153-164.
8. Louis N. Gross, "The Story of My Life," unpublished manuscript, WRHS.
9. Personal communication, Ken Dery, June 18, 2013.
10. Personal communication, Armin Guggenheim, June 19, 2013.
11. Steven Tatar and Denise Grollmus, *The Ohio Knitting Mills Knitting Book: 26 Patterns Celebrating Four Decades of American Knitting Style* (New York: Artisan, 2010), 89.
12. Susan A. Glenn, *Daughters of the Shtetl* (Ithaca and London: Cornell University Press 1990), 97.
13. William Ganson Rose, *Cleveland: The Making of a City* (Kent, Ohio: Kent State University Press 1990 [Reprint of 1950 edition]), 180.
14. Rose, *Cleveland*, 206.
15. Rose, *Cleveland*, 311.

16. Lloyd P. Gartner, *History of the Jews of Cleveland* (Cleveland: Western Reserve Historical Society and Jewish Theological Seminary of America, 1978), 19.
17. Joseph Hays, *Autobiography of Joseph Hays*, unpublished, 1916, 1960, WRHS.
18. Kaufman Hays, Autobiography, unpublished manuscript, WRHS. See also Bob Gries, *Five Generations: 175 Years of Love for Cleveland* (Cleveland, 2014, privately published), 30-31, 43-48.
19. Perhaps not surprisingly, Jews also developed the scrap metal industry into an ethnic niche economy, taking waste and making it usable once again.
20. Gartner, *History of the Jews of Cleveland*, 20. For the distinction between pants and trousers, see Isaac Joseph, "Fifty Years Ago", MS 3886 Joseph & Feiss Company Records, 1847-1960, Container 1, Folder 1, WRHS.
21. MS. 3886 Joseph & Feiss Company Records, Container 1, Folder 1, WRHS.
22. Gartner, *History of the Jews of Cleveland*, 11, 15, 21.
23. The Euclid Garment Manufacturing Co. is the oldest, continuously operating garment manufacturing company in the region. Located today in Kent, the company makes work apparel and protective clothing for a wide range of industries.
24. Rose, 362.

Industry and Immigrants

1. MS 5106 Stanley Garfinkel Oral History Collection, Western Reserve Historical Society, Container 1, Folder 17, Maurice Saltzman, undated.
2. "Knit Goods Company Organized," *The Cleveland Trade Bulletin*, October 1904, 1.
3. Louis N. Gross, *The Story of My Life*, unpublished manuscript, WRHS.
4. "Louis Newton Gross", *A History of Cleveland Ohio*, Biographical, Illustrated, Volume III (Chicago-Cleveland: The S. J. Clarke Publishing Co., 1910), 262.
5. "Importance of Cleveland as a Knit Goods Center," *The Cleveland Trade Bulletin*, September 1905, 1.
6. William Gross, untitled, unpublished manuscript, MS 3823 L. N. Gross Company Records, 1907-1967, Container 1, Folder 1.
7. MS 4711, L. N. Gross Company Records, 1898-1990, Container 5, Folder 78.
8. Abraham Stearns to "Dear Sam & Bertha," November 13, 1900, in Stearns letter copy book, at Jewish Community Federation, Cleveland. Quoted in Gartner, *History of the Jews of Cleveland*, 129.
9. Advertisement, *The Cleveland Trade Bulletin*, August 1904, 4.
10. "Stiff bosoms," *The Cleveland Trade Bulletin*, March 1905, 21.
11. Ibid.
12. "Spring Cloak Season Active with Retailers," *The Cleveland Trade Bulletin*, May 1905, 12.
13. Louis N. Gross, "The Story of My Life," unpublished manuscript, 65, WRHS.
14. Dillon and Godley, "The Evolution of the Jewish Garment Industry, 1840-1940," 40-41.
15. Carol Poh Miller and Robert A. Wheeler, *Cleveland: A Concise History*, 1796-1996 (Bloomington: Indiana University Press, 1997), 82.

16. Miller and Wheeler, *Cleveland: A Concise History*, 199.

17. Mary Barnett Gilson, *What's Past is Prologue: Reflections on My Industrial Experience* (New York: Harper & Brothers, 1940), 66.

18. Bryner, *The Garment Trades*, 47.

19. Glenn, *Daughters of the Shtetl*, Chapter 5.

20. "New 'Clothcraft' Factory," *The Cleveland Trade Bulletin*, June 1905, 1.

21. Lois Scharf, "The Great Uprising in Cleveland: When Sisterhood Failed," in A Needle, A Bobbin, A Strike: Women Needleworkers in America, eds. Joan M. Jensen and Sue Davidson (Philadelphia: Temple University Press, 1984), 161 and John Joseph Grabowski, "A Social Settlement in a Neighborhood in Transition, Hiram House, Cleveland, Ohio, 1869-1912," Ph.D. dissertation, Case Western Reserve University, 1977, chapter 4.

22. Bryner, The Garment Trades, 97.

23. Jacob Applebaum, "From Russia to American Freedom," *Clothcraft*, July 1920, 5, MS 3886, Joseph & Feiss Company Records, Container 5, Folder 10, WRHS.

24. "Those Apprentices, Described by One Who Knows Them," *Clothcraft*, April 1920, 10, MS 3886, Joseph & Feiss Company Records, Container 5, Folder 10, WRHS.

25. Gilson, What's Past is Prologue, 139-140.

26. Gilson, What's Past is Prologue, 66.

27. Green, Ready-to-Wear, Ready-to-Work, 228.

28. "Won't Agree to 'Closed Shop', Employers Say They Will Stand Firm against Cloakmakers," *The Plain Dealer*, August 16, 1904, 4.

29. Scharf, "The Great Uprising in Cleveland: When Sisterhood Failed," in A Needle, A Bobbin, A Strike, 153.

30. "The Life Story of Sidney Walzer: An Oral History by Harley Goldstein, His Grandson," 1983, WRHS, 22.

31. MS 5094 Work Wear Corporation, Inc. Records, Series II, Container 1, Folder 3, WRHS.

32. Marc Frisch, "The H. E. Frisch Knitting Mills Co.," 1, WRHS.

33. Steven Tatar with Denise Grollmus, *The Ohio Knitting Mills Knitting Book*, 2-11.

34. MS 5106 Stanley Garfinkel Oral History Collection, Container 1, Folder 23, WRHS, 1982.

35. Personal communication, Ken Dery.

36. "Enthusiasm for Spring Suit Season High as New Lines Go on Road", *Women's Wear Daily*, December 26, 1934, 26. In MS 4694 S. Korach Company Records, 1898-1987, Container 1, Folder 4, WRHS.

37. *See Remembering: Cleveland's Jewish Voices* (Kent, Ohio: Kent State University Press, 2011), eds. Sally H. Wertheim and Alan Bennett, especially the historical overview.

38. Lloyd P. Gartner, *History of the Jews of Cleveland* (Cleveland: The Western Reserve Historical Society and the Jewish Theological Seminary of America, 1978), 84-85. John Anisfield was the only other Jewish leader on the committee.

39. The Federation for Charity and Philanthropy is known today as the Center for Community Solutions. For distinctions among the Federation for Charity and Philanthropy, United Way Services, and the Cleveland Foundation, see the relevant articles in the *Encyclopedia of Cleveland History* (www.ech.case.edu).

The Place for Progressive Methods

1. Rose Pesotta, *Bread Upon the Waters* (Ithaca, New York: New York State School of Industrial and Labor Relations, 1987), 288.

2. David J. Goldberg, "Richard A. Feiss, Mary Barnett Gilson, and Scientific Management at Joseph & Feiss, 1909-1925," in *A Mental Revolution: Scientific Management since Taylor*, ed. Daniel Nelson (Columbus: Ohio State University Press, 1992), 40-57.

3. Emma S. Brittin, "Two Years of Successful Welfare Work in a Factory Employing One Thousand People", *Human Engineering* 1 (April 1911), 80-86.

4. Untitled report, MS 3886 Joseph & Feiss Company Records, Container 4, Folder 9, October 17, 1914, WRHS.

5. Ibid.

6. MS 3886 Joseph & Feiss Company Records, Container 5, Folder 20, WRHS.

7. MS 3886 Joseph & Feiss Company Records, Container 5, WRHS.

8. "Clothcraft Shops", Report to Detroit Board of Commerce by Boyd Fisher, MS 3886 Joseph & Feiss Company Records, Container 4, Folder 9, WRHS.

9. Untitled report, Service Department, October 17, 1914, 4-5, MS 3886 Joseph & Feiss Company Records, Container 4, Folder 9, WRHS.

10. "The Results of Our English Work", Mrs. Helen Horvath, *Clothcraft*, Volume 1, Number 5, July 1920, 3, MS 3886 Joseph & Feiss Company Records, Container 5, Folder 10, WRHS.

11. "Clothcraft Shops", Report to Detroit Board of Commerce by Boyd Fisher, MS 3886 Joseph & Feiss Company Records, Container 4, Folder 9, WRHS.

12. Ibid.

13. Untitled report, Service Department, October 17, 1914, 9, MS 3886 Joseph & Feiss Company Records, Container 4, Folder 9, WRHS.

14. "Remarks on Housing Conditions of the Joseph & Feiss Employees," MS 3886 Joseph & Feiss Company Records, Container 4, Folder 9, WRHS.

15. Gilson, *What's Past is Prologue*, 210.

16. MS 4787 Abba Hillel Silver Papers, 1902-1989, Container 85, Volume 1, WRHS.

17. William Gross, untitled, unpublished manuscript, 24, MS 3823 L. N. Gross Company Records, 1907-1967, Container 1, Folder 1, WRHS.

18. Quoted in MS 5106 Stanley Garfinkel Oral History Collection, Container 1, Slide Show, "Rags: 100 Years of the Apparel Industry in Northeast Ohio," undated.

19. "The Life Story of Sidney Walzer: An Oral History by Harley Goldstein, His Grandson," 1983, WRHS.

20. "The Life Story of Sidney Walzer," 50.

21. "The Life Story of Sidney Walzer," 26.

22. "Clothing Strike Ends Tomorrow," *The Plain Dealer*, March 18, 1934.

23. "Announce Closing of Kaynee Plants", *The Plain Dealer*, November 13, 1934, 1.

24. "Attack Worker's Home," *The Plain Dealer*, November 11, 1934, 6a and "Kaynee Pickets Stay, Union Says," November 14, 1934, 4.

25. "Pact Ends Strike at Kaynee Here," *The Plain Dealer*, January 12, 1935, 1, 7.

26. "The Life Story of Sidney Walzer," 36-37.

27. Robert Ebert and Shea Monschein, "Paternalism, Industrial Democracy, and Unionization in the Cleveland Garment Industry: 1900-1935: The Case of the Printz-Biederman and Joseph & Feiss Companies," unpublished paper, WRHS, 12.

28. "Intelligent Policing," *The Plain Dealer*, July 1, 1937, 10.

29. Pesotta, 280. For more on Pesotta, see Elaine Leeder, *The Gentle General: Rose Pesotta, Anarchist and Labor Organizer* (State University of New York Press, 1993).

30. Pesotta, *Bread Upon the Waters*, 283.

31. MS 4664 Richman Brothers Company Records, Container 2, Folder 22, WRHS.

32. MS 4561 National Knitted Outerwear Association Records, Cleveland District Records, WRHS.

Fashionable and Affordable

1. "The Clothing Industry Today," *Men's Wear*, January 17, 1969.

2. Frisch, "The H. E. Frisch Knitting Mills Co.," 1, WRHS. For a description of the work done by Italian immigrants for the various factories, see the oral history of Rosaria Cultrona Contini, May 26, 2010, WRHS.

3. *The Majestic Messenger*, September 25, 1942, WRHS.

4. Stephen C. Lampl, "Lampl Fashions Thoughts," August 24, 2012, unpublished manuscript material.

5. Carl G. Lampl to the American Consul, Vienna, Germany, November 1, 1938, family correspondence.

6. Green, *Ready-to-Wear, Ready-to-Work*, 118.

7. Tatar and Grollmuss, *The Ohio Knitting Mills Knitting Book*, 19.

8. MS 5106 Stanley Garfinkel Oral History Collection, Container 1, Folder 8, Sam Janis, February 22, 1982, 17, WRHS.

9. Edward Craig, "The Uniform Picture Gives Way to Rentals," *The News American* (Baltimore, Maryland), February 23, 1967, in MS 5094 Work Wear Corporation, Inc. Records, Series II, ca. 1940s-1996, Container 1, Folder 27, WRHS.

10. MS 4765 Work Wear Corporation Records, 1961-1985, Container 1, Folder 1, WRHS.

11. *The Provo Daily Herald*, June 18, 1973, 15.

12. MS 4765 Work Wear Corporation Records, 1961-1985, Container 1, Folder 1, WRHS.

13. "Work Wear Chief Predicts Good '71 Profit,,*The Plain Dealer*, December 9, 1971, 6-C.

14. Frisch, "The H. E. Frisch Knitting Mill Co.," 3, WRHS.

15. Agnes Harichovszky, oral history interview, September 9, 2008.

16. Art Mayers, oral history interview, 2008.

17. Personal communication, Kay Zuckerman and Dan Zuckerman, September 25, 2012 and November 21, 2013. For additional information on Campus Sweater, see http://vintrowear. wordpress.com/tag/campus-sweater/, accessed November 30, 2013.

18. Art Mayers, oral history interview, 2008.

19. Art Mayers, oral history interview, 2008.

20. MS 5106 Stanley Garfinkel Oral History Collection, Container 1, Folder 17, Maurice Saltzman, undated, WRHS.

21. "Bobbie Brooks: In Quest of the Holy Grail," *Clothes*, Vol. 1, No. 11, August 15, 1966, 22, MS 4764 Bobbie Brooks, Inc., Records, 1939-1992, Container 1, Folder 3, WRHS.

22. Cal Cohen, oral history interview with Marc Frisch, March 21, 2011.

23. Ken Dery, oral history interview, 2013.

Industrial Decline

1. Lauren A. Murray, "Unraveling Employment Trends in Textiles and Apparel," *Monthly Labor Review*, August 1995, 62-72.

2. Personal communication, Fred Jones, November 5, 2013.

3. Personal communication, Tom Adler, August 28, 2012.

4. Ibid.

5. Joseph Schaffner was originally from Cleveland. See Phyllis Dillon, "German Jews in the Early Manufacture of Ready-Made Clothing," *A Perfect Fit*, 68.

6. Olivera Perkins, "Hugo Boss: A Look Behind the Scenes as Determined Workers Fight to Keep Their Plant Open," *The Plain Dealer*, August 8, 2010, http://www.cleveland.com/business/index.ssf/2010/08/hugo_boss_the_story_of_the_bat.html, accessed December 1, 2013 and Olivera Perkins, "Hugo Boss Workers Sign 3-year Contract at Plant that Nearly Closed," March 30, 2012, *The Plain Dealer*, http://www.cleveland.com/business/index.ssf/2012/03/hugo_boss_workers_sign_three-y.html, accessed December 1, 2013.

7. MS 5106 Stanley Garfinkel Oral History Collection, Container 1, Folder 8, Sam Janis, February 22, 1982, WRHS.

8. "The Life Story of Sidney Walzer," 42.

9. Personal communication, Mike Klein, November 14, 2012.

10. Oral history interview, Robert "Buzz" Rosenfeld, June 19, 2012.

11. Mike Duff, "Dollar General Waltzes Bobbie Brooks into Walmart Territory," http://www.cbsnews.com/news/dollar-general-waltzes-bobbie-brooks-into-walmart-territory/, accessed November 30, 2014.

12. Steven Tatar and Denise Grollmus, *The Ohio Knitting Mills Knitting Book: 26 Patterns Celebrating Four Decades of American Knitting Style*.

13. Stephen C. Lampl, "Lampl Fashions Thoughts", August 24, 2012, unpublished manuscript material.

14. MS 5106 Stanley Garfinkel Oral History Collection, Container 1, Folder 1, Sam Janis, February 22, 1982, WRHS.

15. Ron Gottfried, oral history interview, July 3, 2012.

16. Cal Cohen, oral history interview, March 21, 2011.

17. MS 5106 Stanley Garfinkel Oral History Collection, Container 1, Folder 23, David Reinthal, 1982, WRHS.

Conclusion

1. Bart Simon, oral history interview, September 5, 2012.

2. Personal communication, Tom Adler, August 28, 2012.

3. Jennie Miklic Turk, "Richman Brothers", exhibit, Slovenian Museum and Archives, Cleveland, Ohio, 2012-2013.

4. MS 5094 Work Wear Corporation, Inc. Records, Series II, ca. 1940s-1996, Container 1, Folder 27, WRHS.

Richman Brothers, Indianapolis, Indiana, ca. 1940s. (Robert Harger, WRHS)

Bibliography

This bibliography includes a list of individuals who were interviewed in connection with the writing of A Stitch in Time and a selection of the materials available on the history of the industry in the WRHS Research Library. Those interested in the garment industry will also want to consult local newspapers, national trade publications, government labor statistics and works on the industry in other leading centers throughout the country.

Oral History Interviews

Tom Adler

Cal Cohen

Ken Dery

Ron Gottfried

Marc Frisch

Janet Reiter Greenberg

Louis N. Gross

Bill Heller

Jane Horvitz

Fred Jones

Bill Joseph

Steve Joseph

Shirley Kanter

Joan S. Kaufman

Bill Klineman

Gregg Lurie

Keith Lurie

Art Mayers

Howard Nickman

Gary Rand

Charles Rosenblatt

Robert Rosenfeld

Alan Schoenberg

Bart Simon

Myron Stern

Stanley Stone

Selected Published Sources at WRHS

Buyer's Guide to the Cleveland Apparel Market. Cleveland, 1938.

Bryner, Edna. *Dressmaking and Millinery.* Cleveland: Survey Committee of the Cleveland Foundation, 1916.

———. The Garment Trades. Cleveland: Survey Committee of the Cleveland Foundation, 1916.

Buchanan, Thomas. *The Rise of a Manufacturing Class in Cleveland, 1870-1880.* Cleveland, 1989.

Christman, Anastasia J. "Labor Militancy among Working Women during the 1911 Garment Strike," MA thesis, Case Western Reserve University, 1992.

Cleveland Trade Bulletin, 1904-1909, 1910-1913.

Ebert, Robert R, and Shea Monschein. *Paternalism, Industrial Democracy, and Unionization in the Cleveland Garment Industry, 1900-1935: The Case of the Printz-Biederman and Joseph & Feiss Companies.* Berea, Ohio: Baldwin-Wallace College, 2009.

Fashion Book of the Paris Skirt Co. Cleveland: Paris Skirt Company, undated.

Friedman, Blau, Farber Company, *Fifty Years: An Historical Reminiscence, 1883-1933.* Cleveland: Roger Williams Co., 1933.

Gartner, Lloyd P. *History of the Jews of Cleveland.* Cleveland: Western Reserve Historical Society, 1978.

Gilson, Mary Barnett. *What's Past Is Prologue: Reflections on My Industrial Experience.* New York and London: Harper & Bros., 1940.

Gries, Bob. *Five Generations: 175 Years of Love for Cleveland.* Cleveland, 2014. Privately published.

Gross, Louis N. *The Story of My Life.* Cleveland, 1940.

Harrison, Dennis and Greater Cleveland Labor History Society. *Working History: A Manual for Researching and Writing Labor History in Cleveland, Ohio.* Cleveland: Greater Cleveland Labor History Society, 1984.

Hays, Joseph. *Autobiography of Joseph Hays, Cleveland, Ohio, 1838-1916.* Cleveland,   ca. 1960.

Hirschberg, Herbert Irving. *Me.* Self-published. 1981.

Jensen, Joan M. and Sue Davidson. *A Needle, a Bobbin, a Strike: Women Needleworkers in America.* Philadelphia: Temple University Press, 1984.

Joseph & Feiss Co. *The Joseph & Feiss Co. in War and in Peace.* Rochester, N.Y.: L. Hart, 1945.

The Loop. Cleveland: Kaynee Company, 1916.

Miller, Carol Poh, and Robert Anthony Wheeler. *Cleveland: A Concise History, 1796-1990.* Bloomington: Indiana University Press, 1990.

The Majestic Messenger. Cleveland: Majestic Specialties, 1943-1945.

Orth, Samuel Peter. *A History of Cleveland, Ohio Illustrated.* Chicago: S.J. Clarke Pub. Co., 1910.

Rubinstein, Judah. *Remembering: Cleveland's Jewish Voices.* Kent, Ohio: Kent State University Press, 2011.

Smead, Lucille. *Joseph & Feiss in the Earlier Days and Methods and Sources of Data.* Cleveland, 1937.

Tatar, Steven and Denise Grollmus. *The Ohio Knitting Mills Knitting Book.* New York: Artisan, 2010.

III

Manuscript Collections at WRHS

Beryl Peppercorn Papers, MS 3388

Bobbie Brooks, Inc. Records, MS 4764

Bobbie Brooks, Inc. Records, Series II, MS 5157

Cleveland Worsted Mills Company Records, MS 5050

Dalton Company Records, MS 5052

Dorothy and Ralph A. Colbert Family Papers, MS 5161

Federal Knitting Mills Company Records, MS 5051

Ignatz Koenig Papers, MS 3836

Jacob Goldsmith Family Papers, MS 4678

Joseph & Feiss Company Records, MS 3886

Joseph & Feiss Company Records, Series II, MS 5054

Joseph Family Papers, MS 4894

Joseph Family Papers, Series II, MS 5055

Julius Klein Papers, MS 4702

L.N. Gross Company Records, MS 3823

L.N. Gross Company Records, Series II, MS 4711

Leo W. Neumark Papers, MS 4029

Max J. Reiter Papers, MS 5311

National Knitted Outerwear Association, Cleveland District Records, MS 4651

Richman Brothers Company Records, MS 4664

S. Korach Company Records, MS 4694

Serbin, Inc. Records, MS 5053

United National Clothing Collection, Greater Cleveland Branch Records, MS 5032

Wattenmaker Advertising Records, MS 5113

Work Wear Corporation, Inc. Records, MS 4765

Work Wear Corporation, Inc. Records, Series II, MS 5094

Picture Groups at WRHS

Bobbie Brooks, Inc. Photographs, PG 489

Joseph & Feiss Company Photographs, PG 175

Joseph Family Photographs, PG 524

Joseph Family Photographs, Series II, PG 551

Joseph Hays Family Photographs, PG 503

Leo W. Neumark Photographs, PG 319

Richman Brothers Company Photographs, PG 466

Stanley Garfinkel Photographs, PG 576

Wattenmaker Advertising Photographs, PG 578

Appendix A

Garment Manufacturers In Cleveland

John Anisfield Company

Arsham Brothers

Bamberger-Reinthal Company

Bands Waste Material Company

D. Black Cloak Company

H. Black

Bloomfield

Bobbie Brooks

Bradley Knitwear

Alex Brown Knitting Mill

Campus Sportswear

Cashmere Corporation

Cleveland Knitting Mills

Cleveland Worsted Mills Co.

Cohn-Goodman Co.

Dalton

Davis, Peixotto Co.

Erie Dyeing and Processing Co.

Euclid Garment Co.

Excelsior Knitting Mills

Fine Gauge Knitwear Co.

Famous Dress Co.

Favorite Knitting Mills

Federal Knitting Mills

Florian Fashion

Friedman, Blau, Farber

H. E. Frisch

Gottfried Co.

Green Knitting Mills

Green-Haas-Schwartz

The L. N. Gross Co.

D.C. Haber Knitting Co.

Hadley Cashmere Corporation

M. I. Huebshmen

Hibshman Bros.

Isaacson and Kater

Joseph & Feiss

Kastriner and Eisenman (K &E, Kaynee)

Keller Knitting Mills, Keller Kohn

S. Korach Co.

Korrect Coat Co.

Kux Company

Lampl Fashions

Landesman-Hirschheimer

H. A. Lattin Co. (Bloomfield Co.)

Lindner Co. (Lindner-Cox,
      Sterling Lindner Davis, W. B. Davis)

Lion Knitting

Lyon Tailoring Co.

Jerry Lurie

Majestic Sportswear

Meistergram

Nashkin Cloak Co.

National Spinning

North American Knitting Mills

Ohio Knitting Mills

Perla Embroidery

Phoenix Dye Works

Printz-Biederman

Quality Thread Co.

Rich Sampliner Knitting Mills

Richman Brothers Co.

Ritmor Sportswear, Inc.

Root McBride Co.

Rossmor Industries

Serbin, Inc.

M. T. Silver Co.

M & D Simon

Standard Knit

Stone Knitting

Stuart Knitting Mills

Superior Knitting

H. L. Thorman

S. Weitz & Co.

Work Wear

Wovenright Knitting Mills

Appendix B

Chronology Of Garment Manufacturers In Cleveland

This chronological list of garment manufacturing companies was compiled using a variety of sources, including History of the Jews of Cleveland by Lloyd Gartner, The Plain Dealer, Cleveland city directories, manuscript collections at WRHS, The Encyclopedia of Cleveland History and other online sources, and personal communications from descendants of manufacturers. This list is certainly not exhaustive. The goal was to offer additional information about the larger manufacturing companies that left behind traces of their work in the city. In many cases it is difficult to determine the exact details about when a company was founded or when it closed down or about the company's leaders who often spent decades in the garment industry. In addition, tracing the mergers and different names of a given firm, even when possible, is a complicated task. When known, information about mergers and name changes is included. It is hoped that the information offered here may guide readers interested in learning more about specific manufacturing firms.

The list is divided into suppliers, who provided the goods that made the industry possible; knitting mills, which often made a variety of products; manufacturers who made both women's wear and men's wear; manufacturers of women's wear; and manufacturers of men's wear. Companies are listed in order of the year of founding.

Suppliers

1878 Turner Worsted Mill, from 1902 Cleveland Worsted Mill
Founded by Joseph Turner in 1878. The company operated 11 other plants in Ohio, New Jersey, Pennsylvania, New York and Rhode Island. Company President Louis O. Poss shut down the company after a final strike by its workers in 1955. The company's building on Broadway near East 55th Street was destroyed by fire in 1993, after years of neglect.

1903 Arsham Brothers
Founded by the five Arsham Brothers, Shiah, Nathan, Morris, Benjamin, and Sanford, in 1903. Located at 7209 St. Clair. The firm produced fabric cuttings and wool stock. The company received a major blow when a fire was set in their factory in 1934. The company also faced legal complications due to wages for women in 1939. Brothers Sanford, Jerome, Harold, and Alvin were also involved in the family business. Closed in 2001.

1919 Erie Dyeing and Processing Co. (including Cashmere Corporation of America and Hadley Corporation)
Founded by Ben Haber, an attorney, in 1919. The first plant was in Brooklyn, Ohio, before expansion to Cleveland. The company's main purpose was to dye and bleach cotton and woolen and worsted yarns. Rudy Adler was a chemist with Erie Dye who developed a special dehairing process for dehaired cashmere and camel hair. Haber later created a supplementary company known as the Cashmere Corporation of America, which sold sweaters. The company started another division called the Hadley Corporation, meant to produce higher quality knitwear. In 1958 Richard Haber took over Hadley Corporation which was later sold to Dalton and Erie Dye was sold to the Arsham brothers.

1921 National Spinning Co.
Founded in 1921 by the Leff and Misheil families. Their first plant was established in Jamestown, New York. Later the company expanded to both Cleveland and North Carolina. The firm produced worsted yarns and dyes. It became a public corporation in 1968 until all of its extended shares were bought by the corporation in 1981.

1922 The Quality Thread Co.
Founded in 1922 by Morris Berman. The firm's first products were apparel items. As the market shifted, the company expanded to include industrial sewing markets in its manufacturing list. Vice President Robert Flacks bought the company in 1992. The firm was still in operation in 2014.

1932 Isaacson and Kater Button Co.
Founded in 1932 by Isaacson and Leon Kater. The company produced and supplied both dyed and undyed buttons, as well as elastic, laces, tapes, pins, snaps and sewing hooks. Brothers Phil and Leonard Goldberg, who met Leon Kater in the military during World War II, were involved in the business after the war. The company could not compete with outsourced prices and was sold in 1995 to John Hirsh and shut down permanently soon after.

1933 Meistergram
Founded by Eugene B. Meister in 1933. Meistergram was at one point considered the largest manufacturer of monogram embroidery machinery. The company sold and leased its machines to a number of different companies as a way of self-promotion. Eugene Meister ran the company until its closing in 1977.

1946 Perla Embroidery

First documented in 1946, the company was founded by Herbert H. Perla. The firm was located in a single story brick building, found on the east side of East 23rd Street between Payne and Chester Avenues. Perla manufactured various trims, styles and mended emblems, as well as other embroidery.

1957 Phoenix Dye Works

Formally known as the Phoenix Steam Dyehouse, the company was originally founded by Anton Susen in Chicago in 1896 and relocated to Cleveland in 1957. Central products were cotton, hemp and linen yarns with the intent to be used not only in clothing but in other household items as well. The company expanded to include a potato chip plant, while also continuing plants related to the manufacture of dyed yarn on cones and skeins for the knitwear industry. Located at 4755 West 150th St. Later owned by Fred Jones and his father.

Knitting Mills

1883 Friedman, Blau, Farber

Founded in 1883 by Herman Friedman, who was later joined in running the company by William Blau, Adolph Farber and Isadore Whitelaw. This firm was the only fully integrated knitting mill in Cleveland, having developed its own dye house, box factory and knitting machines. The company supplied knitted outerwear for all ages and genders. Located in 1920 at Perkins Avenue and East 37th Street. The firm closed in March 1939.

1901 Rich-Sampliner Knitting Mills

Founded in 1901 and led by S.S. Sampliner, W.E. Sampliner, N.I. Rich and S.G. Kennedy. The company manufactured products such as knit goods for men, women and children, knit cloth, athletic suits, bathing suits, cardigans, novelties, mufflers, sweaters, coats and letter jackets. Sampliner was sold in 1905. The company went bankrupt in 1928.

1901 Standard Knitting Mills

Founded in 1901 by European immigrant O.F. Schmidt. The firm produced clothing for men, women and young boys, including sweaters and coats. Schmidt was assisted by O.N. Fishel and O.I. Bauer in running the company. O. N. Fishel's son Richard was also active in operating the company in the 1950s and 1960s.

1905 Federal Knitting Mills

Established in 1905 by Julius Feiss of Joseph & Feiss and Louis Hays of Kaynee, among other leaders in the industry. The firm was created with the purpose of producing knit items such as sweaters. The firm also made and supplied fabric to the garment manufacturing industry. Located at 2860 Detroit Ave. The company closed after the strikes of 1937, with the explanation that it could no longer afford production.

1906 Bamberger-Reinthal Company

Founded in 1906 and run by Gus Bamberger and his brothers-in-law Sol and Manuel Reinthal. The company produced men's, women's and children's sweaters as well as caps and hockey caps. The firm supplied knit helmet liners, camouflage nets and navy watch caps and sweaters to the military during World War II. The firm was sold to Koracorp Co. in 1969 and shut down in 1977. Later principals of the company included David Reinthal and Arthur Reinthal and Stephan Ross. Ross bought equipment from Bamberger-Reinthal for the development of Rossmor Industries, another knit-goods manufacturer.

1906 Green-Haas-Schwartz Co.

Established in 1906 with the help of E.D.W. Haas, E.E. Schwartz and I.H. Green. The firm manufactured upscale men's, women's and children's knit goods, sweater coats and mufflers. Located at Euclid and East 57th Street.

1906 United Knitting Mill

First publicized in 1906, the United Knitting Mill was located at 1258 West 4th St. United Knitting manufactured sweaters and knit scarves throughout the early twentieth century. Run by Julius W. Dentsch.

1908 [1912?] Wovenright Knitting Mills

Founded in 1908, the firm was run by J. Norton as president and F. Norton as secretary and treasurer. The company made men's seamless hosiery.

1910 Favorite Knitting Mills

Max and Sarah Cohen and Charles Wien founded Favorite Knitting Mills in 1910. The company specialized in outer wear, such as sweaters, coats, cardigans, hoods, caps, mufflers and mittens as well as other novelties.

1911 Keller Knitting Mills, Keller Kohn

Founded in 1911 and run by W.M.H. and F.C. Keller as well as N.F. Dryfoos and G.W. Hirst. One of the leading manufacturers in the 1920s, the company produced sweaters and coats for men, women and children. The Sterling label of women's coats was sold at modest prices. Arthur Dettelbach was involved in the business in the mid-twentieth century.

1912 Lion Knitting Mill

Founded in 1912 by Louis and Harold Ensten. The firm's first product was the varsity sweater. During World War II the company designed and produced knitwear for the U. S. Navy and Army. Locations included 1011 Power Ave. and 3256 West 25th St. near Meyer Ave. James Hibshman joined the firm in the early 1930s and was associated with the firm for more than 50 years. He also served for a time as chairman of the board. The Hibshman family, including Norbert and Lawrence Hibshman, controlled the company from 1971 until its closure in the spring of 1990.

1912 D.C. Haber Knitting Co.

Founded in 1912 by D.C. Haber, with the help of M.L. Goldstein, Fred Desberg and Dave Warshansky. The firm mainly produced mittens and gloves. Both D.C. and Archie Haber oversaw production of the factory through its later years.

1920s Lampl Fashions

Joseph Lampl started Lampl Knitwear in the 1920s (precise year of founding unknown), with the help of Carl G. Lampl. The company went on to become Lampl Fashions, known for both knitted and standard clothing for men and women. The company assisted the war effort during World War II by manufacturing parachute parts for the military.

1922 Pontiac Knitting Mills, from 1926 Campus Sweater Co.

Established by Samuel S. Kaufman and Loren B. Weber as Pontiac Knitting Mills in 1922. Name changed to Campus Sweater Co. in 1926. The company was one of the largest manufacturers of casual clothing for men. Moved to Ridgewood, New Jersey, before being absorbed in 1968 by Interco, Inc. from St. Louis.

1927 Stone Knitting Mills

Founded by Harry Stone and Walker Woodworth to manufacture clothes for both men and women. The company was taken over by Stone's son-in-law, Leonard Rand. The company produced materials for the U.S. military during World War II. In 1947, Rand transitioned the company and renamed it Ohio Knitting Mills. The company continued to be family run until its closing in 2004. Located at Stanton Avenue until its move to East 61st Street and Euclid. The buildings that housed the company in both locations have been torn down.

1929 H. E. Frisch Knitting Mills Co.

Founded by Harry Frisch in 1929 after Harry left his position at Rich-Sampliner following that company's bankruptcy. Frisch developed a business of distributing both fabrics and clothing items. The company's success was mainly contingent on the new machinery brought in to ease production and expand its range of material and pattern styles. The sons of Harry Frisch, Marc and Jerry, later joined the family business and were active in operating the company until the 1970s.

1931 Excelsior Knitting Mills

Founded in 1931 by Bert Haas and Herman Klein, Excelsior Knitting Mills manufactured women's and men's sweaters. Like other manufacturing companies, supplied the U.S. Army with camouflage nets, wool army sweaters, and caps during World War II.

1932 Green Knitting Mills

Established in 1932 and run by S.M., L.R., and I.H. Green, Green Knitting Mills specialized in manufacturing children's sweaters, dresses, headwear, cardigans, and polo shirts.

1947 North American Knitting Mills

Formerly known as Frederick Kinkel & Sons, North American Knitting Mills was moved to and established in Mansfield, Ohio, in 1947. Founded by Johann and Frederick Kinkel, and later run by Frederick's son, Jacob Kinkel, who moved the company to Cleveland and subsequently changed the company's name. Originally producing children's clothing, the company moved on to include men's and women's sweaters. The company was sold in 1990 and was dissolved soon after.

1947 Ohio Knitting Mills

Leonard Rand, the son-in-law of Harry Stone, transitioned Stone Knitting Mills into Ohio Knitting Mills in 1947. Gary Rand became president of the company after his father's death in 2001. Located at Stanton Avenue until its move to East 61st Street and Euclid in 1970. The factory ceased operations in 2004 after the building and land were sold to the city of Cleveland for redevelopment in 2004. The buildings that housed the company in both locations have been torn down. The East 61st Street parcel will be developed by University Hospitals for a clinic for women and children.

1949 Fine Gauge Knitwear Co., later Dalton of America

Founded in 1949 by Arthur Dery and Maurice Saltzman. The company changed its name to Dalton of America in 1956 as a way of reorganizing the company. The firm initially produced only women's cashmere and woolen clothing items but later expanded to produce other knitted outerwear. Arthur Dery took on the company as sole proprietor in 1957. The firm was shut down in 1986.

1960 Stuart Knitting Mills

Created in 1960 by Albert Abady, an employee of Dalton. The company manufactured fashionable sweaters but shut down three years later from lack of sales.

1960s Alex Brown Knitting Mill

First publicized by The Plain Dealer on October 6th, 1962; year of founding unknown. Founded by Alex Brown and located at 6116 Broadway. The firm produced sweaters and other knit goods.

1974 Rossmor Industries

Established in 1974 and run by Stephan and Anita Ross. Ross was born in Germany and served in the British army during World War II. He came to Cleveland in 1962. Ross was also affiliated with Bamberger-Reinthal. The company had a license agreement with the NFL to make hockey caps with team insignias. Manufactured knitted headwear and scarves in Twinsburg, Ohio.

Men's Wear and Women's Wear

1877 M. T. Silver Co.

Founded in 1877 by M.T. Silver. The firm was one of the first to encounter difficulties with labor. A strike caused a major production setback in 1896, with negotiations at a standstill. While manufacturing, the firm produced coats for men, women and children.

1878 Landesman-Hirschheimer

Established in 1878 by Jacob Landesman and A.W. Sampliner. They were assisted by Isaac Levi as vice president, B. Lowenstein as treasurer, and Harry New as secretary, with Landesman acting as president. The company manufactured cloaks and suits.

1882 John Anisfield Company

Founded by John Anisfield, an immigrant from Vienna and a former employee of the D. Black Cloak Company. The firm was located at East 22nd Street and Superior Avenue. Later, in 1909, Anisfield erected a building at East 9th Street and Huron Road. Anisfield retired in 1923. Beyond his business life, Anisfield served as president of Mt. Sinai Hospital and the Infants' home, in addition to establishing Camp Anisfield, a camp for Jewish working girls. His daughter Edith Anisfield Wolf established the Anisfield-Wolf Book Awards in 1935 to recognize literary work focusing on issues of social justice.

1883 H. Black & Co.

Founded in 1883 by Herman Black, and later managed by his son Morris Alfred Black. The company manufactured Wooltex coats and suits, and was once considered one of the largest coat and suit manufacturing firms in the world.

1903 Hibshman Bros.

Founded by Hibshman brothers Louis, Ben, Sam, and William in 1903. The firm sold wholesale hosiery and underwear and was located at 2025 East 9th St. William Hibshman died in 1943. Louis Hibshman retired in 1942. The company was sold in 1954.

1915 Cleveland Overall Co., later known as Work Wear

Established in 1915 by Samuel Rosenthal. Built to manufacture work clothes, mainly industrial. In 1919 the firm absorbed the National Railway Overall Company. The company made a profit selling and renting uniforms for other work corporations and later became a pioneer in the industrial laundry business. Leighton Rosenthal, son of Samuel, led the firm through the mid- to late twentieth century. Locations included 3600 East 93rd St. and 1768 East 25th St. Acquired by Paine Webber Capital in March 1986.

1918 M & D Simon

Founded by Max Simon (1888-1968) in 1918. Simon was the first president as well as one of the founders, of the Jewish Community Council in Cleveland. He served as president and owner of M & D Simon until his death in 1968. M & D Simon specialized in double knits. Donegal was one of the company's brand names. Eddie Simon and Sydney Simon eventually took over the company's operations. The company was later a division of Bobbie Brooks Company, which later became part of Pubco Corporation.

1923 Nashkin Cloak Co.

Founded by Fishel Nashkin, a Jewish Polish immigrant, in 1923. Nashkin was also a prominent Yiddish-speaking actor and monologist in Cleveland. Located on Superior Avenue, the company manufactured cloaks for both men and women. Nashkin retired, along with his business, in 1958 upon his move to Florida, where he continued to pursue his Yiddish acting career.

Year of founding unknown S. Weitz & Co.

Founded by Louis S. Weitz. Louis acted as president of the firm, although he was located in the company's New York office, while David E. Weitz served as secretary and treasurer in the Cleveland office. The firm was known for manufacturing Westberry overcoats. In 1953 the firm combined with Jos. H. Cohen & Sons, and in 1959 the firm moved out of Cleveland.

Women's Wear

1874 D. Black Cloak Co.

Founded by David Black in 1874. Black was an immigrant from Hungary, having arrived with his family in the early 1850s. Black owned a garden market between Wilson and Woodland Avenues, and from there he decided to start manufacturing women's cloaks for profit. Black died in 1880, shortly after his business took off. His nephews, Joseph and Louis Black, succeeded him in business. Another nephew, Herman Black, founded H. Black & Co. in 1883.

1893 Printz-Biederman Co.

Established by Moritz Printz, his sons Michael and Alexander, and his son-in-law Joseph Beiderman. The company manufactured women's and children's clothing of all kinds. The firm grew exponentially by the early 1900s, acquiring the Sampliner Company in 1905. Locations included 102 St. Clair, 71 Bank St. (1213 West 6th St.), and 1974 East 61st St. Max Reiter of Ritmor Sportswear Co. took over in 1954. The company closed in 1978.

1898 The L. N. Gross Co.

Founded by Louis N. Gross, an immigrant from Russia, in 1898. Gross managed the company until his death in 1941. The company was left in the hands of his sons, Nedward N., William V., and Julius, and son-in-law Milton E. Reed. The firm's main headquarters was at 1220 West 3rd St. Additional production sites were located in Kent, Ohio, and Fayetteville, Tennessee. The name of the company was changed to Bradley Sportswear, Inc., in 1984.

1901 Cohn-Goodman Co.

Founded in 1901 by L. Goodman and A. A. Cohn. The firm was located at 99 Bank St. and specialized in women's clothing. In 1904 all of Cohn-Goodman's 250 workers refused to enter the establishment because of a union dispute.

1902 S. Korach Co.

Founded in 1902 by Sigmund Korach, the firm manufactured ready-to-wear dresses and skirts for women. After various sites, the company located permanently at 2400 Superior Ave. Family members involved included the Korach brothers, Charles, Leo, and Benjamin, and Sigmund's son Arthur. The company closed in 1935. The building was then leased to the Weinberger Drug Company, later known as the Gray Drug Company. The building was converted into a warehouse after 1977. In 2014 the building became home to both an art gallery and a printing firm.

1906 Lattin-Bloomfield Co.

Founded by H. A. Lattin and Sol Bloomfield, a former employee of the M.T. Silver Company. In 1917 the company moved to West 9th Street. Skirts were the primary product of the firm. Members of the National Cloak, Suit, and Skirt Manufacturers' Association. H. A. Lattin was president, Sol Bloomfield vice president, and E. A. Overbeke secretary.

1913 Bloomfield Co.

Founded in 1913 and located at 2122 Superior Ave., the Bloomfield Co. manufactured women's dresses. The firm was operated by Sol Bloomfield, also part owner of the Lattin-Bloomfield Co. He also served as president, J. Bloomfield was vice president and E. A. Overbeke was secretary.

1918 Majestic Sportswear

Majestic Sportswear was founded in 1918 and run by the Klineman brothers: Dave, Emery and Irwin. The company manufactured and sold skirts, blouses and sweaters. Majestic moved to New Jersey in the early 1950s.

1927 Famous Dress Co.

Established in 1927 with James Dworkin as president and Max Gevelber as both secretary and treasurer. Once located at 2530 Superior Ave. Manufactured and sold women's dresses.

1927 Gottfried Co.

Founded in 1927 by Emil Gottfried. Made and sold women's dresses, in sizes produced for women of European descent with body sizes different than the average woman. Gottfried was assisted by Harold Oster as vice president, and Ronnie, Martin, Carl and Larry Gottfried. The business remained successful and was sold out of the Gottfried family in the 1980s.

1939 Ritmor Sportswear, from 1960 Bobbie Brooks

Established by Maurice Saltzman and Max Reiter in 1939 under the name of Ritmor Sportswear. Saltzman became the sole owner of the company in 1953. The name of the firm was changed to Bobbie Brooks in 1960. At that time the company sold clothing aimed at junior sized women and eventually expanded to include older women. The company was absorbed into the Pubco Corporation in 1985.

1943 Serbin, Inc.

Founded in 1943 by Lewis I. Serbin and M. John Serbin. Made women's sportswear, especially golf apparel. The company, as well as the Serbin family, left Cleveland for Florida in 1951. The company officially went out of business in 1991.

1959 Florian Fashions

Founded by Jerome Lurie in 1959. Lurie had previously been a comedian in the Catskills. In the beginning, Lurie designed his own dresses and sold them directly to vendors. Florian Fashions succeeded by having a business partnership with the Gottfried Co., producing women's dresses in all manner of sizes. The two companies eventually split due to economic differences. Florian acquired Dalton in the late 1980s and held fashion lines under the Dalton name. Gregg, Keith and Ken Lurie, sons of Jerome, were all active in the family business.

Year of founding unknown Kux-Bleiweiss Company

Founded by Louis and Martin Kux in Cleveland, with Martin as president and Louis as vice president. The company was originally known as the Plus Dress Co. The firm sold dresses shaped for half-sized women. With the addition of a business partner, the firm became the Kux-Bleiweiss Company.

Men's Wear

1845 Joseph & Feiss Co.

Kaufman Koch moved Koch & Loeb, a wholesale clothing store, from Meadville, Pennsylvania, to Cleveland in 1845. The company sold piece goods to tailors and manufactured its own brand of clothing, contracting with small ethnic shops. Developed first into Koch, Goldsmith, then in 1873 became Goldsmith, Joseph, & Co. The firm became known as Joseph & Feiss in 1907. Locations included 642-702 St. Clair St. and 2149 West 53rd St. Felix S. Mayer served as president of Joseph & Feiss from 1931 to 1957. Richard Adler was president of Joseph & Feiss in the 1960s, before becoming head of the Greater Cleveland Growth Association in the 1970s. Merged with Phillips-Van Heusen Corp. in 1966 but retained its own name and operations. Hugo Boss bought the Joseph & Feiss plant in 1989 and continued to make luxury men's suits well into the twenty-first century. In March 2015 Hugo Boss announced plans to sell its plant on Tiedman Road to W. Diamond Group Corp., a manufacturer of Hart Schaffner Marx suits.

1847 Davis, Peixotto Co.

Founded by Benjamin Franklin Peixotto and George A. Davis. The firm manufactured thousands of uniforms for the Union during the Civil War. A downshift in production followed business success during the Civil War. The firm closed in 1867. Peixotto became American Consul to Romania in 1870.

1876 Euclid Garment Co.

Founded by brothers Simon and David Rosenblatt in 1876. Produced men's pants, overalls and shirts. The company occupied three floors on St. Clair Street. During World War II, Euclid Manufacturing expanded to produce women's coveralls for defense plants. The company relocated to Kent in 1952. In 2008 the company was renamed Euclid Vidaro, a combination of the first letters of the last names of business partners Henry Vircant and Ed Davis and Charles Rosenblatt. The company continues to manufacture items for the aerospace, medical and pharmaceutical industries in 2015.

1879 Richman Brothers Co.

Established by Henry Richman in Portsmouth, Ohio, the company moved to Cleveland in 1879 and made and distributed men's suits, hats and other furnishings. In 1907, Richman's sons, Nathan, Charles and Henry, took over the business and opened their own retail outlets in the process. Located on East 55th Street, George Richman led the company throughout the mid-twentieth century. The company was considered the largest clothing chain in the United States in the 1950s. F.W. Woolworth Co. purchased the company in 1969. The Woolworth Co. closed the Richman unit in 1992.

1888 Kastriner and Eisenman, later known as Kaynee (from K & E)

Established by J. Kastriner and Charles Eisenman. Manufacturer of boys' clothing (blouses). Incorporated as Kaynee, after various name changes, in 1914. Managed by Robert L. Hays as both president and treasurer, and Roy A. Ferguson as both vice president and secretary after 1914. Located at Aetna and Broadway.

1922 Lyon Tailoring Co.

Founded in 1922 at 845 Prospect Ave. The company grew rapidly in its first few months, opening another two plants within 16 months of its first opening. The firm manufactured all types of men's suits, topcoats, tuxedos, sports models and jazz models, all of which were ready to order.

Appendix C

COMPANY CONNECTIONS

David Black Cloak Company

John Anisfield worked at the D. Black company for six years before starting the **John Anisfield Company**.

Moritz Printz was a designer at the D. Black company. Printz later joined with Biederman to create the **Printz-Biederman Company**.

Herman Black, David Black's nephew, started the **H. Black & Co**. firm in 1883.

Rich–Sampliner Knitting Mills

A.W. Sampliner paired up with traveling cloak salesman, Jacob Landesman, to form the **Landesman-Hirschheimer Cloak Co**. in 1878.

Harry Stone was a floor-sweeper and Walker Woodworth was a plant supervisor, both at Rich-Sampliner. Together they created **Stone Knitting Mills.**

Harry E. Frisch was a salesman at Rich-Sampliner, and later went on to start the **H.E. Frisch Knitting Mills**.

Harry Stone's daughter, Ruth, married Leonard Rand, the owner of **Ohio Knitting Mills**. Rand took over Stone Knitting Mills from his father-in-law years after.

Harry Stone's sister, Pearl Stone, married H.E. Frisch.

Before founding Federal Knitting Mills, Louis Hays worked for and helped turn the Turner Manufacturing Co into the **Cleveland Worsted Mill**.

Joseph Hays' daughter, Bertha, married Charles Eisenman, founder of **Kastriner and Eisenman**, later called Kaynee.

Charles Eisenman was first cousins with Charles S. Rosenblatt, whose family founded the **Euclid Garment Manufacturing Co**.

Julius Feiss (**Joseph & Feiss**) and Louis Hays (**Kaynee**) teamed up to found Federal Knitting Mills as a co-partnership in 1905.

Louis Hays' wife, Jessie Seligman Feiss, was the niece and adopted daughter of Julius Feiss.

Federal Knitting Mills

Maurice Saltzman began working for **Lampl Fashions** in 1934, when we was sixteen years old.

Joseph Lampl worked at the Federal Knitting Mills until 1920s, when he founded **Lampl Knitwear**, while his brother Carl opened **Lampl Fashions**.

Arthur Dery worked at Federal Knitting Mills until buying part ownership of **Excelsior Knitting Mills**.

Dery teamed up with Maurice Saltzman of Bobbie Brooks to create the **Fine Gauge Knitwear Company**. The name was changed to **Dalton of America** in 1956.

Maurice Saltzman and Max Reiter, a salesman from Lampl, started **Ritmor Sportswear** in 1939. The name was later changed to **Bobbie Brooks**.

Albert Abady, creator of **Stuart Knitting Mills**, worked for Dalton before starting his company in 1960.

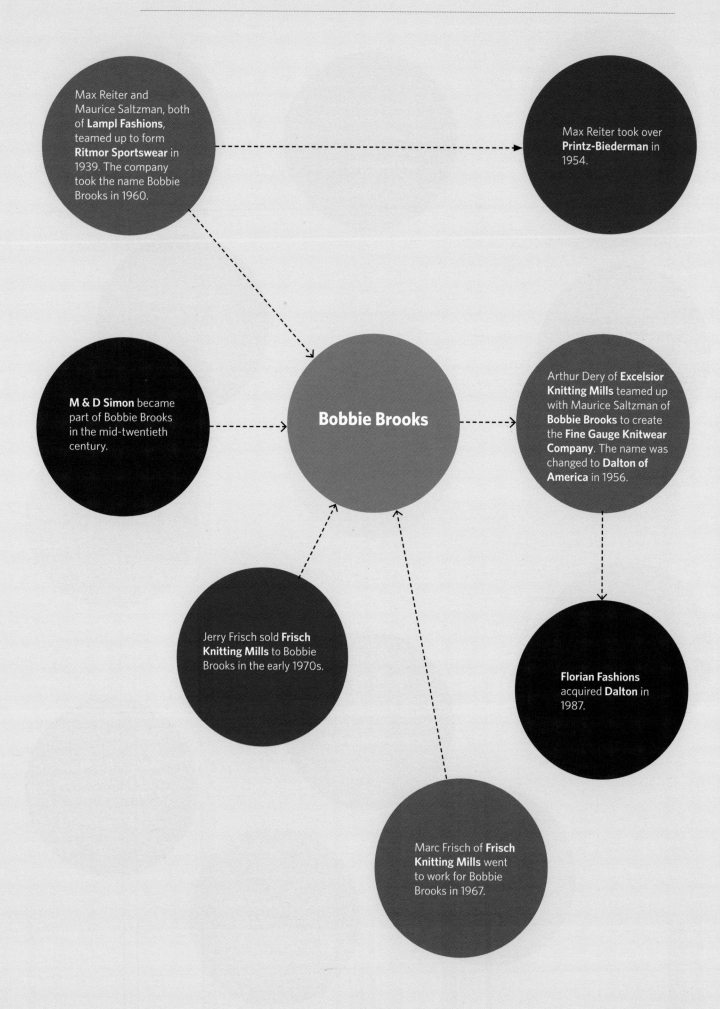

Max Reiter and Maurice Saltzman, both of **Lampl Fashions**, teamed up to form **Ritmor Sportswear** in 1939. The company took the name Bobbie Brooks in 1960.

Max Reiter took over **Printz-Biederman** in 1954.

M & D Simon became part of Bobbie Brooks in the mid-twentieth century.

Bobbie Brooks

Arthur Dery of **Excelsior Knitting Mills** teamed up with Maurice Saltzman of **Bobbie Brooks** to create the **Fine Gauge Knitwear Company**. The name was changed to **Dalton of America** in 1956.

Jerry Frisch sold **Frisch Knitting Mills** to Bobbie Brooks in the early 1970s.

Florian Fashions acquired **Dalton** in 1987.

Marc Frisch of **Frisch Knitting Mills** went to work for Bobbie Brooks in 1967.

Index

A NUMBER IN ITALICS INDICATES AN ILLUSTRATION.

Advertisement for Dalton, undated. (Arthur, Ken, Jim, and Bob Dery, WRHS)